A TRILOGY OF
GOD'S STORIES

Kisses from Heaven

BOOK TWO

Unique, Inexplicable, Extraordinary, and Supernatural Tales from the Heart of a Miraculous God

"Publish His glorious deeds among the nations. Tell everyone about the amazing things He does."
—Psalm 96:3, NLT

C. B. Caleb Woodworth, MD

with My Dear Wife and Co-author, Emily Woodworth

Disclaimer: These true stories are seen as factual through the eyes of the one who lived and chronicled them, so are based on the author's experiences and opinions, expounded by his personal interpretations, and wide open to others good will observations. However, before we deliberate in love, dear one, it is wise to remember that a man with an experience is rarely at the mercy of a man with an argument. Maybe never here. Names and places may have been altered to protect the innocent.

Praise for *Kisses from Heaven, Book Two*

"*Kisses from Heaven* is a book hard to put down. Caleb's experiences and the way he shares them are fascinating. I love sharing those stories with others, and now that I have the book, I can keep all the facts straight. This book is a tremendous testimony to the power, accuracy, and gentleness of the Holy Spirit and will inspire you to watch and listen for opportunities to live a Spirit-led life."

—**Jerry Murphy**, Apostle, Groundskeeper, and Altar Dweller, Moriah Ranch, Poplar Bluff, MO

"Decades ago, Restoration Ministries helped prepare this book's authors for service to the brokenhearted, afflicted, and needy. Who could have foreseen the plethora of heavenly intercepts, here depicted as God Stories, that Holy Spirit would lead them through as testimonies to the goodness of God in the land of the living and divine proof that Jesus is the same yesterday, today, and forever? Is walking in day-to-day wonders with Holy Spirit what the Lord has for you? Get ready for ways to help you find out."

—**Pastor Ed Glaspey**, Founder/Director, Restoration Ministries, Junction City, Oregon

"*Kisses from Heaven* by Dr. Woodworth is an inspiring collection of life stories that beautifully showcase the goodness of God and the active role of the Holy Spirit in our daily lives. Through heartfelt narratives—both engaging and uplifting—he illustrates how God's love touches even the smallest moments, reminding readers that no event in our lives is too trivial for God's attention. If you are seeking encouragement and a deeper understanding of God's love, faithfulness, and miraculous working power, *Kisses from Heaven* is a must read."

—**Lori Salley**, Founder/Director of Operations, Show Mercy International

"Terminally-ill Susan was bedfast and too sick to seek healing at a Benny Hinn meeting. Not to be denied, Caleb and I, in a School-of-Tyrannus-like move, carried her long-wasted Jesus T-shirt for a laying on of hands by Benny. That prayer had to wait, however, until Caleb's shorter than Kitty Hawk flight into the lap of a lady in the front row and his time of being 'not drunk as you suppose' were over. Only then could Susan, clothed in Benny's freshly anointed burial garment, fly away into the healing arms of Jesus at daybreak. You must read this hard-to-believe story, 'A Pair of Susans,' to believe it. Thirty-plus years later, it is still hard for me. And I was there!"

—**Susan Riscili**, Friend to the Broken and Mother of Israel,*
Junction City, Oregon
*co-authors' and many others' unanimous opinion

Dedication

To Holy Spirit, without whom we get nothing done (John 15:5).

To my Proverbs 31 wife, Emily, without whose love,
encouragement, and patience this work would
still be the stuff of dreams (Prov. 18:22).

To every soul kissed by Heaven in this book who came back to
give to God the glory due His name (1 John 4:19, Matt. 10:8b).

Contents

Acknowledgments

Bob Ridings, Chuck Estabrook, Charlie Holcomb, the USAF Ubon Team, Crows, Pastor Mac Wright, Elmer Reaser, a young Bangkok nursing student, Father Kelly, Mildred Eastburn, Carol King, Al Perna, two pushy angels, Holy Spirit, Susan (Brennan) Riscili, Benny Hinn, Eddie Williams, an elderly lady evangelist in Grants Pass, Emily and her sisters, an old wooden boat lover in Sequim, Shay Martin, the "Swede," Dad (Hugh Woodworth), Pastor John Bowers, Hugh Woodworth Jr., MD and wife Karen, Katie Woodworth Richards, Shelby Jones, the Show Mercy International Team, Pastor Denny Cline, Evangelist Rodney Howard Brown, Evangelist Carl Madison, Apostle Jerry and Sandra Murphy, Hugh and Martha Martin, my faithful wife Emily, Gary Jeter (computer scribe and friend) and Beth Lottig of Inspire Books (my coach and so much more). Bless all, along with those who have shared their podcasts, radio time, and pulpits, for your participation in bringing the Lord glory due His name. For those "Flown West" (aviator lingo for having passed), give our love to Jesus.

Preface

Expect this book to provoke divergent opinion, even controversy. Truth does that—ask Jesus. God Stories often go against the grain of traditional American Christianity, pushing back the worn-out arguments that Holy Spirit, His giftings, and His divine interventions are not for today but ended when Apostle Paul (allegedly) lost his head in Rome. Then, as commonly accepted, all we need do is preach the gospel, adhere to sound biblical teaching, gloss over the book of Acts, and explain away all things Holy Spirit to keep the faith alive and growing.

Are there problems here? Several. Wouldn't purging Holy Spirit from our Holy Spirit-inspired Bible eliminate a Holy Spirit-inspired Bible, expunging Holy Spirit from biblical teaching abolish the originator of biblical teaching, and excluding Holy Spirit from our Spirit-led walk deny divine interaction with the only God on Earth?

Wouldn't dissecting the Bible of its otherworldly origin and our supernatural actor from His supernatural acts deny both the kingdom of Heaven, the King, and His gospel from intervening in the affairs of men?

Then, wouldn't reducing or removing Holy Spirit and His otherworldly gifts, acts, and interventions from our Bible, based on assumptions and conclusions rooted in the traditions of men—for which Jesus had little use (Mark 7:8)—seem a little risky? Who knows if those assaults on the Word of God and God the Spirit Himself might be considered blasphemy to put us on Jesus' "Depart from me, I never knew you" list (Matt. 7:21–23), especially if we keep assigning His gifts to the devil (Matt.12:22–24), who curiously, we are led to believe, is not for today either.

We could ask Thomas Jefferson why he deleted everything supernatural from the French Geneva Bible and King James versions of the Gospels to render his own interpretation, the Jefferson Bible (the life and morals of Jesus of Nazareth extracted textually from the Gospels), which remains in print. Jefferson, a deist who favored reason over revelation, rejected many Christian miracles, including the resurrection.

By Jefferson's connecting his name to an altered Bible, he presumed the entirety of God's Word was no longer immutable, requiring some explanation at the White Throne Judgment, we might suspect.

Do you recall when deified Jesus emptied Himself of equality with God by laying aside the use of His divine attributes—position, privilege, and power (Phil. 2:5–8)—to enter an extended period void of supernatural activity? Then, when His equality with God and divine attributes were again quickened during His Holy Spirit baptism (Luke 3:22), that divine refreshing instantly led to a pair of supernatural interventions by a Holy Spirit-empowered Jesus: (1) a private three rounds of verbal fisticuffs turned TKO that left Satan in the wilderness looking for a rematch and (2) a public 720 gallons of freshest water turned finest wine at the Wedding at Cana embarking Jesus on a ministry of miracles.

So, let's be reminded that so much of our Holy Spirit-deprived American Church is going nowhere in its spiritual shrinkflation while the worldwide Spirit-led body of Christ is claiming volcanic growth, the gifts of Holy Spirit flourishing, and seeing more supernatural miracles than ever. We earlier mentioned diverse opinion and controversy. Well, here we are in that proverbial nutshell, but with a well-tested way to crack it.

Jesus learned early on that He needed to prove His gospel, so signs and wonders became His answers. After Cana, the multitudes followed

Him not so much for His well-received gospel (John 7:46) as the way He gave it teeth with miracles (Matt 9:33). He publicly concluded this, "Unless you people see signs and wonders, you simply will not believe" (John 4:48). Since then, people have changed no more than Jesus, who said He was the same yesterday, today, and forever (Heb. 13:8). From Thomas the Doubter needing to touch the Lord's wounds to believe (John 20:28) to the elderly grandma's command, "Show me the Beef," in the classic Wendy's commercial, we see humankind's need to see proof before committing to any earthly undertaking.

Understandably, Jesus chose not to profess being Messiah when John the Baptist sent his disciples to ask if He was the One... "or do we look for someone else?" (Luke 7:19. Instead, the Lord instructed them to tell John about His miraculous works (Luke 7:22).

So, for good reason, the Lord did not change His unchangeable gospel to make it more seeker-friendly but left us His same and "greater works" to confirm it (John 14:12). Then He sent us a Helper (Holy Spirit) to make that happen (Acts 1:8). Why? Maybe the Lord knew we would need more miraculous help to convince others of His gospel during our ungodly days than during His. ("Miracle": An extraordinary event manifesting divine intervention in human affairs, Merriam-Webster Dictionary, 1831).

What you are about to read are excerpts from the eight-five-year-life of an everyday Christian, a patriotic American citizen and taxpayer, Naval aviator, Vietnam veteran, medical doctor, VA clinic director, ordained pastor, long-term-short-term missionary, and restoration (i.e., inner healing) minister, who, along with co-laborer, wife, and intercessor Emily, have found that Jesus loves to weave His wonderous ways (unique, inexplicable, extraordinary, and supernatural God Stories) often incognito, always purposefully, and commonly at the eleventh hour through the lives of believing Christians to convince unbelievers of His gospel. Freely you received, freely give (Matt. 10:8) has always been a motto of our Savior (Luke 6:38). Forgive us when our tales are somewhat more modest than the Lord's.

The Lord asked us in 2002 to chronicle our God Stories to pay them forward to the body of Christ and those requiring added proof that Jesus is alive and well on planet Earth (Heb. 13:8), His gospel is true today as ever (John 17:17), and He is still at work to eagerly offer His salvation, gifts of Holy Spirit relevant to present times, and a divine, intimate, and relevant personal relationship with Him for all who believe (Eph. 2:8).

Let me whet your appetite with the following mini Kiss from Heaven, which may create a conundrum. Will you see this God Story as coincidence, good karma, kismet, luck, or chance—all anathemas in the life of a Christian where God orders every step (Ps. 37:23–24), or as a personal encounter choreographed by our loving God?

Can you believe that a young woman abandoned by, estranged from, and incommunicado with her biological father for an entire twenty-year span was living a life so filled with hurt, anger, bitterness, and hatred that, in desperation, she finally sought help? No doubt you can.

Can you believe, by the end of her ministry session with Holy Spirit (well, we were there too), she had repented of her many sins of anger, found forgiveness, healing, His truth to set her free, and then, suddenly, experienced a fervent longing to reconcile with her father after long years of hate and discontent? Harder? Sure.

Can you believe this? Twenty minutes after Emily and I left her home came a knock on the young woman's door where her father stood asking for forgiveness and pleading for a fresh start with the daughter lost to him for two decades.

No? Then you do not know our eleventh-hour Jesus (Ps. 37:23-24).

Yes? Then read on, pilgrim, and discover the Lord is impartial, plays no favorites, is no respecter of people (Acts 10:34) but is ready and willing to prepare you for your own "Kisses from Heaven," God

Stories, believable and contemporary testimonies to bring Jesus to life in both yours and others' worlds as Savior and Lord. If meaningful encounters brought the lost to Jesus, shouldn't they do the same today?

All we need do is ask, believe, learn to wait patiently while about our busy days, become alert listeners amid their noise, and when Holy Spirit prompts us in our secret places, heed and obey Him instantly, joyfully, and completely.* Then, when "Kisses from Heaven" follow as God Stories from our lives testifying to the goodness of God in the land of the living (Ps. 27:13), remember to pay them forward. Why? Simple; they are not our stories, Christian; they are the Lord's. So freely receive and freely give. Then, when God's love stories begin to flow from your life, watch for hard hearts to soften, stiff necks to turn, prodigals to return, and His chosen to come home to Jesus.

Introduction

This is a book of God Stories. That bold statement demands explanation. Who speaks for God? Not this man. So, let's try to define a God Story not by its content, for as we will see, each story speaks for itself, but by what criteria qualifies it to bear such a heady title. Is there a higher experience for a born-again Christian than to become a privileged moving part in a wonderous story created, choreographed, and christened by the Father, the only One who can guarantee Himself the glory He deserves? Let us see what it takes, at least from the eyes of this mere human.

God's Intimate Presence

God's intimate involvement defines a God Story. Remove Father's hand, and there is no story, at least not one worth telling. Test that statement; read a God Story. Then, remove all the elements in it that make it unique, inexplicable, extraordinary, or supernatural. The result? The story ends! It becomes an unfinished event, inconclusive and void of any meaning on earth or glowing significance in Heaven. A God Story excluding God becomes a hollow collection of thoughts, words, or actions, a narrative with no divine worth or purpose.

God's Wondrous Character

A God Story always portrays the character and works of God as wonderous. What has happened in the story makes it difficult to describe or discuss without reaching beyond the ordinary and into the sublime. Applying uncertain or ill-defined words like luck, kismet, karma, serendipity, coincidence, or chance to explain a God Story only tarnishes the story's credibility and diminishes its meaning. Father's thumbprints, often hidden throughout a tale, are enough to confirm its place as a God Story.

God's Benevolent Intent

God Stories are uplifting, encouraging, edifying, or comforting for those both participating in the story or those listening to it further on as a testimony. God Stories leave no doubt as to Father's pristine character (proving who He is) and His infinite power (displaying what He does). Even more, they reinforce His loving intent toward us, which always supplies listeners with grateful hearts, elevated faith, and awe, if not worship for His inalterably benevolent heart and beneficent ways.

God's Lifelong Lessons

Lessons well learned remain as jewels mined from the residual of any passing God Story. Whether with knowledge gained relevant to a specific moment or wisdom applicable to life over the long haul, the Lord rarely transits our lives without teaching His tailored truth. All we need do is slow down and allow Holy Spirit to unwrap the truth waiting for us in any God Story, whether arising from our own or others' testimonies.

God's Glory Due His Name

A God Story preeminently exalts God for who He is, what He does, and only by way of a moment He considers worthy of His glory. So, what greater privilege for a Christian than to be invited to play a living role in a God Story where He is at His glorified best, the unabashed purpose is to bring Him glory due His name, which becomes an inevitable, unsolicited "Kiss from Heaven" for any believer taking a privileged part, and, finally, brings an unchangeable living testimony of God's majesty even to those of us participating vicariously.

Questions

Do you question God's desire to bring you a story for His glory? How can you be certain that you are ready to hear Him? Are you a waiter and listener with ears to hear? Are you ready to obey instantly, joyfully, and completely* when you do? Are you ready for God to intervene in your most mundane of daily events or in the middle of the most impossibly demanding and inconvenient of situations? Are you willing to drop everything at a moment's notice to have your life turned upside down by God interrupting you in the most uncomfortable, inflexible, or humiliating of ways?

Are you then willing to deny yourself, pick up your cross, and follow Him?

Are you willing to lay down your life for your Friend? Are you willing to enter an inferno for making your decision to accompany Him at all costs? How about bearing accusations of irresponsibility for not being a Christian, being a Christian in name only, a sociopathic liar, a hyper-spiritual whacko, unhinged, or demon-possessed? Ready to lose friends? Good friends? Family? Close family? Church family? Face jealousy? Condemnation? Rejection? Abandonment? Persecution?

We need not go further, do we? But we could. And Jesus did. So, if you are not ready to follow Him down this narrow highway, faithfully keep doing what you are doing that pleases Him. Though all His highways are narrow, and but one leads to the Father, there are many paths through His kingdom. If you are ready for a wilderness journey into another promised land of milk and honey, adventurous "Caleb," let Him know, be on the alert, keep your toothbrush on call, and your backpack packed. Then, prepare yourself for the most remarkable years of your life. Always be aware—God is no respecter of persons, impartial, and more than ready to deliver you a "Kiss from Heaven" as an arrow to your evangelical quiver as a testimony to His glory.

Postscript

Throughout this tome's writings, you will come across dependable "Postscripts" designed to give Holy Spirit a chance to comment or the author (more often scribe) to enter his ten cents' worth. Then, occasional lighthearted tales may seem to fall outside the parameters of a God Story. I admit to considering such delights only after added thought, which you may consider adequate as a "Kiss from Heaven" as we do.

Still, please honor these tales as God-given (meaning they are purposeful) and Heaven sent to serve as testimonies to (1) the goodness of God in the land of the living (Ps. 27:13), (2) enable both Jesus, His gospel, and His words to become relevant to our times and believable as lights to a progressively darkening world, and (3) equip individual Christians to carry unique, inexplicable, extraordinary, and supernatural testimonies to build faith for themselves, convince others, and prove the gospel as apostacy grows, churches close, and our Bible is outlawed.

No one participating in a God Story will ever be the same and will commonly be ruined for the ordinary but equipped with a living testimony to build their own; they are not our stories, Christian—they are the Lord's. So freely receive and freely give. Then, when God's love stories begin to flow from your life, watch for hard hearts to soften, stiff necks to turn, prodigals to return, and His chosen to come home to Jesus.

*from *Forever Ruined for the Ordinary* by Joy Dawson (Thomas Nelson, 2001).

Introduction from Emily

Living a life of Kisses from Heaven has been an adventure as the wife of a man who is obedient to the call of God, day or night, rain or shine, snow, or—you understand. My husband is a true servant of the Lord. When we started this journey twenty-seven years ago by marrying, leaving our nine-to-five jobs, selling our home, and moving into a small motorcoach, it was, admittedly, a stretch for me. But what a marvelous stretch it became—and all because we dared lay down the things of this world, pick up the cross of Christ, and follow hard after Him.

We quickly became acutely aware of Holy Spirit's voice and His unspoken interactions with us as we continued to diligently seek and, soon it seemed, find Him everywhere we turned. Then, every glorious adventure was followed by another.

As you read this book, keep in mind such a lifestyle can be a tad unpredictable, if not chaotic, to say the least; although it has not always been easy, it has absolutely been fulfilling. Whether or not you choose to follow a path like ours, know that God is always with us, always speaking, and forever working. It is simply up to us to make a conscious effort to make ourselves available and aware of His purposeful laboring in our lives and the lives of those around us.

If we seek Him with all our hearts, He will soon be found, and all because He helps us get out of our own ways to make room for His.

A Pair Of Pushy Angels (1983)

After three years of private practice, we bought a deserted, ransacked, one-story, flat-roofed office building in downtown Cottage Grove, Oregon, on a land sales contract from a local couple who seemed happy to get 12 percent interest on their note. Little wonder when you contrast that rate with ones we have seen to date. An exquisite eyesore with a perfect location, the little rectangular building, the color and shape of an oversized Velveeta cheese box, bordered a quaint, well-kept, but rarely used city park to the west of the property while the Coast Fork of the mighty Willamette River wandered serenely around its perimeter to the north. The building had potential but was a "piece of work," a little colloquialism that proved to be more like a prophecy.

A busy local contractor, my pal Al Perna, took mercy on our little clinic family. Between him, a handful of our patients gifted with amazing carpentry skills, local artisans, and my own blessed children, staff, and friends, together we dove into gutting and rebuilding the little jewel from stem to stern. The local hospital, at the time conveniently remodeling its own X-ray facilities, gave us a dozen used lead-lined wall panels along with a couple of expensive lead doors, thousands of dollars of used material for a mere twenty-five-dollar donation. Following the installation of an X-ray unit of dubious age along with a basic laboratory, we furnished each of three exam rooms with flawless secondhand office furniture and medical equipment handed down from a worn-out internist begrudgingly retiring from a forty-year practice in Portland.

Our team completed the entire project, to our dismay and gratitude, within a three-week window and without a hitch . . . well, except for one afternoon when the plumber, painter, carpet layer, and I retired a little earlier but much giddier following the injudicious use of lacquer to finish the cabinets by our contractor, Al. Later, when clear-headed, we unanimously agreed our early egress that day was due less to the celebratory effects of our breathing the lacquer's intoxicating fumes than the more sobering effects of Al's unsolicited and ceaseless bellowing of the "Wedding of Figaro" during the whole unseemly affair.

Undeterred, we opened the refurbished and resurrected little clinic with a grateful heart and visible fanfare to years of challenging but satisfying family practice in the heart of wood products America. Life as a solo general physician chocked full of rarely consistent adventure looked like this: surgery, if scheduled, at 7:00 a.m. followed by rounds on hospitalized patients, office hours from 9:00 a.m. to late afternoon or early evening, and, finally, evening rounds. Liberally sprinkled throughout the day were quick trips to deliver impatient babies, urgent calls to the emergency room, visits to the high school locker room as team doctor, running to the activities of my five children, training for long-distance road races as a desperate way to find a few minutes of solitude, meeting my pal Al once a week for breakfast, making it to Wednesday night and Sunday morning church services, and rarely grabbing a quick lunch at the Vintage Inn, a local eatery. All this said, I infrequently arrived home for supper (a fact that I regret and a decision I would not make again), rarely slept through the night without an interruption by an apologetic but legitimately needy patient or nurse and struggled to get out of bed every morning of my entire work life.

A Peterbilt Surprise

This Monday had been no different. Eyes full of sleep and body crying for just one more horizontal moment, I stumbled downstairs to the kitchen for a jolt of leaded java before leaving for the office. Ferried earlier by their "swimmer mom" to early practice, left me alone to inadequately console our five poochies. Weekends, gratefully, were set aside for family, although the children would complain that Saturday swim meets, home-based work parties, or Sunday church services devoured them before they could get a taste. The weekend in my rearview mirror and running a little late, with a "McDonald hot" cup of coffee in Big Brown, my wrinkled stick shift Chevy Suburban, we rolled down the steep driveway as a preface to entering Government Road while marveling as I did most mornings at the glorious expanse of Dorena Reservoir stretched out lazily to the north, fog rising from her somber and still-slumbering surface. "At least someone was getting a little rest," was my daily hackneyed retort before thanking the Lord for this breathtaking way to build a grateful heart for His creation before starting another hectic day in mine.

Slicing through a dense forest of giant Douglas firs, Government Road was little more than a reworked rural paved logging path with few shoulders or guard rails to shield a vehicle from its sudden turns and steep embankments. That day, like most Oregon winter days, was dark, drab, wet, and chilly. The highway was slick, so I lingered at the mouth of our driveway until a loaded log truck on the way upriver to the Stewart mill thundered past, shaking "road wash" all over Big Brown before we took the road. Heading northwest while working my way through the old boy's gears to settle him into an easy fifty-miles-per-hour cruise, I put in my favorite Reba Rambo cassette. (Anyone remember Reba?)

A parade of mill-bound log trucks flew by, heading in the opposite direction, each rudely disturbing the Suburban with windy backlashes and more mini-showers purloined from the wet roadway. Within minutes, we approached the former Young Life Christian Camp, strategically situated a couple hundred feet from a blind curve marking the final descent from the reservoir's dam. There was no warning. None. Coming off that hill from the dam and plunging deeply out of control into the hairpin turn at its base was an empty log truck carrying its trailer, tires in a losing struggle to hold on to the greasy curve, and, sickeningly, as a squatter occupying Big Brown's and my entire lane. For us, there was no wiggle room. The fog line to our right was less than two feet from a treacherous unguarded thirty feet of near vertical drop into old-growth timber, which left no shoulder for any evasive maneuvers. But there it was, a mighty Peterbilt, bearing down on us, fifty feet away and so close I could read the manufacturer's emblem on its grill.

"Well," I mused with unequivocal certainty, "here comes today's main event." Foot jammed upon the brake, Big Brown and I, hydroplaning along that rainswept highway, quickly dissolved what little time left by deliberating between a face-to-face meeting with the looming log truck or breaking the surly bonds of earth with a short flight into a cavernous roadside abyss guarded by a legion of giant Douglas firs. It took no deliberation at all to see that either choice presented a one-way ticket to Heaven.

It was inexplicably, then, and in less than the blink of an eye, that our out-of-control gargantuan adversary, his grill nearly filling Brown's windshield and within "spittin' distance" of our unscheduled tête-à-tête, performed the inconceivable.

Deftly as any skilled Olympian, that monster truck, with no perceptible alteration in speed or heading, slid sideways a full ninety degrees from its established path, leaving Big Brown and me in full possession of our rightful lane as the Peterbilt took the opposing one. Screaming by, that behemoth caused the overmatched Suburban to convulse violently once again in its wake.

What I saw during that briefest of moments revealed how that Peterbilt log truck made such an improbable athletic move to avoid a deadly destiny: Two huge but nearly transparent "men" with long blond hair, one pushing against the side of the Peterbilt's enormous chrome-plated radiator and the other aft of the driver's door, had shoved that massive truck ninety degrees from its established path into the opposing lane within a millisecond. How about that as a unique way to jumpstart your day?

Postscript

Thanking the Lord for His mercy, I mentally pinched myself to make sure I was alive. The whole episode was over nearly before it began. What share of my nine lives had been used up in that closest of close calls? There had not been time to feel fear, so my heart was not racing. Nor did I require a "time out" to catch my breath. Reacting to this incident was reminiscent of how similar "near misses" during my years as a Marine aviator flying off carriers or in Vietnam—except, without saying, at different altitudes.

The truth was, I continued nonchalantly with my day and put the whole event in that metaphorical rearview mirror. Understandably, that curve beyond the former Young Life camp held significance for me from that day forward. It was not so sentimental a one, however, to prevent my applauding the State of Oregon when it widened Government Road with substantial shoulders, installed Herculean guardrails, straightened out and properly banked that blind curve, harvested enough of those big firs to see a country mile, and, finally, christened that renovated highway South Shore Drive on what I had always believed the west side of the reservoir. No need to comment, friend.

Now, each time I take a trip down memory lane to Dorena Reservoir, I cannot help but vividly relive my Kiss from Heaven, where an unscheduled intervention by two giant guardian angels repositioned a rogue, out-of-control Peterbilt log truck on old Government Road bringing not only new life but new meaning to an especially endearing Bible scripture: "Are they not all ministering spirits, sent out to render service for the sake of those who will inherit salvation?" (Heb. 1:14). Can I hear an Amen? You have mine, Jesus.

QUESTION: Where is the Kiss from Heaven in this God Story?

ANSWER: Do we need to waste ink on clarifying that answer? Didn't think so. How about we use up lots of praise for a watchful Heaven? Amen.

The Roberts Rebellion (1952)

After requesting and receiving literature from scores of kit boat companies, followed by hours poring over specifications and prices, I chose the Roberts Company's runabout kit, which shortly found its way into our breezy basement on Elm Street. It was there my father and I planned a busy winter piecing this beauty together. Predictably, his meticulous and plodding work ethic collided with my "that's close enough for government work" attitude. (This was before Ritalin, or I might have been its first patient.) Predictably, it was not long before our father-son bonding experience (I thought we were building a boat) would turn into just another contest between two discordant wills. Agreeing to disagree, I went to play neighborhood football, basketball, and, finally, a little baseball while my dad suffered through six months of hand drilling and countersinking brass screws through cedar plywood into oak ribs.

Spending just enough time in the basement each weekend to precipitate an impasse, I would go my way as my father, steadfastly but independently, pursued my dream. A supremely handsome fourteen feet of racing boat, remarkably sturdy and built beyond specifications, greeted me early one spring day, the day my father was finished (in many ways, I might add), and my independent work could begin.

Somehow, my "*comme ci, comme ca*" attitude with the assembly process had not translated to my assignment as a painter. Within two weeks, a perfect specimen rested on the cold basement floor. Waiting for those two months to pass before we strapped the big Mercury Mark 15 to that baby was a lifetime. Then it was Skaneateles Lake, beware. Sadly, that prophecy was to bear fruit.

A Little Tail Chase with a Big Ending

What more could a hyperactive (I would have preferred "adventuresome") thirteen-year-old boy ever want? Nothing. The years have stolen our first "flight," but let us vividly share a more memorable one that followed. On as fine a Saturday afternoon imaginable, having left not only our dock behind but my dad raking the beach without my help, the Roberts was cutting through glassy seas heading south toward a large point of land and a friend with a similar runabout. Meeting under the warm summer sun on this still day, there began a tail chase with me in pursuit. Now both our crafts were highly maneuverable but mine quicker.

Most smaller racing boats had crash throttles using a spring-loaded handle to control engine speed. Once released, the handle would open automatically, causing the engine to go promptly to idle. The Roberts throttle did not have that safety feature. Might you see where this is going? Summer weekends were a busy gaggle of boats crisscrossing each other's paths and wakes. A wise boater kept alert to avoid collisions. As the day faded, fewer vessels were active in our area, so colliding with another boat became less of an issue. Collision with another boat's wake, however, was a different matter. Out of nowhere, I stuck a large "sneaker" wave left behind by a heavy craft long departed. Without warning, the Roberts was ninety degrees to the water, on her left gunnel, and well on her way to flipping over. One thought filled my mind: "Don't lose the boat."

Almost a reflex, I kicked the craft away, instantly finding myself submerged in the cool, dark waters of the lake. Popping up like a bobber, there was the runabout's transom gathering distance between us with no crash throttle or driver at thirty-five miles an hour. My first inclination? Save the boat!

When Preteen Minds Think Alike

While furiously beckoning my friend, the errant Roberts craft was scribing a giant circle intent on intersecting my present position in a matter of seconds. Diving to six feet to watch its propeller carve out a path directly above my head, I quickly surfaced and struggled aboard my friend's waiting craft. We frantically mapped a course of action; the plan was to intercept our quarry at a predetermined point on the circle and wait until the boat rocketed past. At that precise moment, I would spring from the bow of my friend's boat into the Roberts' cockpit. That insane plan, devised with preteen ingenuity, failed brilliantly as our estimated point of intercept moved fourteen treacherous feet aft the one predicted.

There, squarely perpendicular to the transom of my friend's boat, the Roberts' bow delivered a lethal blow to its victim's stern. The force, violent enough to shear four bolts holding the motor's powerhead to its midsection, instantly sent the former to Davy Jones's locker. Scuttled, we lay dead in the water as the Roberts circled relentlessly toward its next assault. Happily (maybe a less-than-optimal word choice), the collision changed the runabout's course to take us temporarily out of the circle and harm's way. Scanning the area, a growing group of concerned bystanders lined the shore while a scattering of passing boats sought safety in deeper water to take in the unexpected theatrics.

Then, my heart leapt with hope. Friends of ours, Chuck, a middle-aged cottage owner, and Charlie, his son-in-law, valiantly mounted their own independent offensive in a stout sixteen feet of wooden Thompson boat powered by a twenty-five-horsepower Evinrude engine. With Chuck driving from the aft seat and Charlie in the forward cockpit, they swiftly launched to put an expected end to the insolent runabout's shenanigans. Regrettably, in one very unexpected moment, they did.

Their craft, now a part of the Roberts' infamous circle of destruction, became caught in its own wake (crippled by the Evinrude's cavitation) and could not avoid a direct blow amidships by the crazed runabout. The impact caused the entire Roberts and its Mercury engine's propeller, generating thousands of RPMs to leave the water and rocket over the Thompson. In the front seat, Charlie, folding forward into a pretzel, still took a glancing hit by the flying rudder, which tore his shirt and inflicted a large bruise across his exposed back. The mortally wounded Thompson, a twelve-inch gash exposing her ribs and private parts to the elements and all of us nearby, quickly filled with water to the gunnels and, long vacated by her two dazed passengers now safely resting in a near shock-like state on the shore, awaited her own death knell.

Its course once again changed by the most recent collision, the sturdy little Roberts boat switched tactics. Whether puffed up over her own recent conquests or merely needing a more formidable challenge, the runabout moved into shallower water bordering a vertical limestone cliff.

Generating larger and larger waves near the rock face, the unrestrained little boat rode them like a surfer off Diamond Head to repeatedly leap airborne from tight circles to strike the rock face with fury. Then, crashing into the waiting water below, the runabout endlessly repeated its ongoing assault against the cliff. Crushed and heartbroken by all the day's events, I became further devastated by the punishment my own craft was now inflicting upon itself.

No Hero's Homecoming Today

Then, as quickly as this nightmare began, it was over. The Roberts had run her Mercury Mark 15's fuel tank dry. I could finally feel my body. It was vibrating. Collective sighs went up along the shoreline, followed by claps and wolf whistles. The growing row of vessels that had paused in deeper water for the unheralded performance added their cheers and horns from afar while moving away into the lengthening shadows of this lovely summer's afternoon. My boating friend's father towed the Roberts with me aboard to our cottage, where he graphically detailed the afternoon's perilous events to my attentive dad, rake still in hand. By this time, I could not stop shaking. Predictably, my father was at once apologetic that his son had caused this inconvenience to our neighbors and destruction to their property. When he discovered the full extent of the damage, his face turned a peculiar shade of red. That was never a good sign for me.

Feeling very unheard (look, it was not like I planned this caper), my mother took me to the sleeping quarters and gave me a half grain of codeine, which put the boy to sleep until morning. Well, Dad's insurance covered all the damages to the Thompson, the medical bills for Charlie's negative X-rays, and replaced my friend's engine with a brand-new Mercury outboard along with Chuck's Thompson. As for the little Roberts runabout, that exquisitely overbuilt craft assembled by my ultra-conscientious father survived the onslaught with but scrapes to her brass bow plate. That was it. Nothing more. Didn't that day become a testimony to my father's skills as a carpenter (maybe a tad less as a dad), considering the carnage the little boat and I had left behind? So ends my saga of the Roberts' rebellion. "Kisses from Heaven" received. Count the multitude.

Postscript

An accident is an event happening by "chance," so says the dictionary. If one assesses blame for a true accident, then "chance" is the sole suspect. Regrettably, "chance" is often intangible and as elusive and easy to bottle as the wind. That does not work for humans. When damage happens, be it an outboard motor sentenced to Davy Jones's locker, a mortal blow dealt a treasured family boat, a physical injury requiring medical care, or emotional pain suffered from the trauma of uncontrollable circumstance, victims so often want tangible justice. Tangible damage demands tangible tribute. "That is why we have insurance," you might say. True. But what about the intangible injury from irreplaceable losses like a life free from a traumatic memory, an ongoing sense of inherent peril, betrayal of trust, or a nagging lack of self-worth; does insurance cover such insults? Sometimes, it tries, but most often fails.

Look, where emotional pain or loss arises from accidents caused by humans, circumstances, or even "chance," the human heart meets an irreconcilable force: Justice applied seems more like justice denied. The human heart is rarely satisfied with applied justice. Humanity's unsolvable enigma with pain or loss is not only the inevitable sense of inadequate justice served but a failure to grasp that suitable justice to the wounded heart is rarely based on objective truth but more on subjective emotion. Rarely is enforced law, an insurance award, or a judge's decision tailored precisely enough for every wounded or brokenhearted victim, their friends, or family.

Isn't that why Jesus said from the cross, "Father, forgive them for they know not what they do" (Mark 23:34). Was it not because our merciful Lord and Savior knew there was no adequate, proper, or acceptable justice for the crucifixion of the Son of God and that even eternal punishment in hell would fall far short? For certain. So, Jesus understood what His executioners were facing. He also recognized those crucifying Him did not understand who they were murdering. Nor did they see the sin in it. Had we asked them, we would have been told they were simply following orders and doing what they had been assigned.

The heart, Jeremiah said, is deceitful above all things; who can know it? (Jer. 17:9). Yet the Bible states that each of us knows the law of God in that same heart, and our conscience and thoughts either accuse us of error or commend us for truth (Rom. 2:15, paraphrase). Did those crucifying Jesus know what they were doing was wrong? So says the Word. But did they know He was the Son of God? And did they know what they were in for? Not likely. What a conundrum. What is the solution? Again, Jesus was the way and had the answer. *

When we bypass the need for justice by choosing not to take offense or by forgiving other humans by dropping one already taken ("You owe me nothing, and I owe you nothing"), it is because we grasp this: If the hearts of the guilty were not deceived but sensitive to God's Word, Jesus' heart, others' pain and needs, and their own conscience (Rom. 2:15), they would not commit the offensive acts to begin with. How the Lord made peace with His crucifiers, or my father made peace with his son (after the accident and all its fallout) would be identical: "Mercy triumphs over judgment" (Luke 6:37). When we refuse to let offense take root or choose forgiveness to set our perpetrators, "chance" itself, and ourselves free from the requirements for justice, we allow mercy (not giving punishment deserved) and grace (giving pardon not deserved) to govern our lives. Only then will everyone involved be set free from self-imposed prisons of offense, unforgiveness, and sin.

You may recognize this story, but it is worth repeating. Emily and I ministered to a younger Christian woman estranged from her father for twenty years; during that entire period, she had not seen or spoken with him. Wounded, angry, and vengeful for his abuse, neglect, and abandonment of her as a child, as a devoted Christian adult, she came to understand her need to forgive her father before receiving forgiveness for herself (Matt. 6:14–15). Under conviction by Holy Spirit (John 16:8), she was convinced she needed both. During our ministry, she would go deeply to the roots of her pain and, without the specifics, not only forgave her father for his offenses (in her heart where she had demanded justice) but also herself (for her own sins of judgment and unforgiveness).

Instantly, she hungered for reconciliation with her dad. But how could she find him? Within twenty minutes of our departure, she later reported, came a knock on her front door. There stood her father confessing his failings, asking forgiveness for all the years of separation and pain, and pleading with her to make things right. She was so astounded and grateful to the Lord she could barely speak. We reminded her that to heavenly Father, there is nothing more precious than reconciliation and that He had given His only Son on that cruel cross to eradicate His differences with us and ours with one another. So, was it surprising that Jesus would patiently wait twenty years to arrange an immediate reunion between an earthly father and his daughter the moment they met His requirements for forgiveness? Not at all. With a willingness to drop her offenses and forgive her father, our young friend had not only opened the door of her home to her now-forgiven father but the door to her own now-forgiving and forgiven heart. Reconciliation complete, and "Kiss from Heaven" received.

*Christ knew who He was: God's sinless lamb, perfect, complete, lacking in nothing (Jam. 1:4), holy, blameless, and beyond reproach (Col. 1:22), and obedient Son on a mission to please the Father. So, knowing His flawless identity and exactly who He was, Jesus had no reason to pick up an offense (stumble) during His passion, which negated the need for Him to forgive His executioners. Instead, feeling compassion let Him ask Father (whose no-murder law was in the process of being broken) to forgive those executioners (based on the

Lord's present redemptive work of taking their punishment on the cross) by extending mercy (not giving them what they deserved) and grace (giving them what they did not deserve). Jesus understood that with seared consciences, His torturers were unaware of the heinous crime they were committing. These were Romans, who did not accept He was the Son of God (until, in one instance at least); He had given up the Spirit (Mark15:39), and their cruel behavior (which was to them merely part of their assignment and military culture) broke God's law requiring justice.

QUESTION: Where are the Kisses from Heaven from this God Story? There are several. Here are two.

ANSWER: (1) Why the Roberts craft, when striking my young friend's boat, did not leap from the water while he stood erect and directly in its path (as it later did when ramming the Thompson) is inexplicable. Surely, the little guy would have died or suffered grave wounds when we consider how the crazed boat, its propeller turning over 5000 rpm, later missed big Charlie (scrunched forward and sitting much lower in the front seat of the Thompson) by the width of a tiny rudder. Incomprehensible? Well, except by Him who is, gratefully, so often so. (2) Then, isn't it wonderful to understand that when we truly know who we are in Christ Jesus, we not only become personally unoffendable but also simultaneously compassionate for the forlorn, lost, sad state of others? Have you asked Jesus to show you how eternally blessed we are with Him in heavenly places while His foes, looking to offend us, face endless torture in hell without Him? Doesn't your newfound compassion drive you to see your foes saved from the wrath of God and instead to eternal life with Him (John 13:3), even as Jesus saw His co-sufferers on the cross, those who at that moment were crucifying Him, and the rest of us who merely looked on?

"Can-Do" Can Do You In (1967)

There has always been a healthy level of competition between the military services. In country, during the Vietnam conflict, that spirit became heightened between Air Force pilots and Marine aviators. The Air Force, well recognized for its daily heroic and sacrificial sorties over North Vietnam, was still challenged by a solid reputation earned by the "on-call," life-saving, close air support from Marine attack pilots in I-Corps abutting the DMZ. On the ground, "dogfaces" and "jarheads" loved the Marine "jet jockeys," especially those deadly precise A-4E Skyhawk attack drivers, who, like swarms of hornets carrying napalm, bombs, rockets, and twenty-caliber cannons, would descend to "save their bacon" time after time when threatened by superior numbers of Viet Cong and North Vietnamese forces. Not that the rest of the Navy Department did not fly its fair share of missions into the north (via US Navy carrier-based aircraft) or the Air Force supply much-needed cover to the South, but, in our world of Chu Lai, Marine close air support was the unchallenged king of the hill and deservedly so.

Whether the following is a current practice or not, I cannot verify, but at one time, the Marine Corps showed its "can-do" mettle and team spirit by returning funds to the Department of Defense at the end of each fiscal year while the Air Force went to Congress with holes in its pockets to plead for more funds every fourth quarter. Why? Because it had run out of gas money and could not afford to fly. How about that for something of little use: a grounded Air Force? It did not take an Einstein to contrast the gulf between that "can-do" Marine attitude and a "can't do" Air Force political philosophy. Do we feel hackles arisin' in the wild blue yonder?

Look, when welcomed to a Marine base in the States, you could easily find Soviet-style, third-world cinder block buildings, tin hangers, and near-barrios for base housing. If you visited an Air Force base, you understood where their money went. It was a military Beverly Hills, Shaker Heights, and Marco's Island all rolled into one. Okay, I will admit to a little hyperbole, but anywhere you went, the Air Force was flush with every advantage known to a man in uniform. Little did I realize that one dark night—well, let us move on.

Class Warfare

That portrait of the inter-service class struggle did not change one iota with the war's onset when Chu Lai, Vietnam, became Marine Aviation's true poster child. On that air base upon the dunes bordering the South China Sea, ground pounder tents, primitive dwellings, and aviator open-air plywood hooches embellished by palm-frond-thatched roofs made up much of the landscape.

Then, constructed from sheets of "skid proof" (I am being facetious) two-by-twelve-foot sections of aluminum alloy matting (weighing 144 pounds per sheet) joined upon constantly shifting and unreliably reinforced sand, Chu Lai's runway suffered constant degradation from C-130 Hercules transports weighing 184,000 pounds; contrast that tonnage to the 24,500 pounds per loaded A4E Skyhawk for which those runways were primarily installed. That perilous roller-coaster runway was intermittently but poorly lit at night by a handful of ancient bulbous Seabee hand-me-down kerosene construction flare pots, alternately flickering in monsoon rains but snuffed by typhoon winds. Aircraft taxi lights on takeoff and landing mitigated that problem but gave Viet Cong snipers nestled in the vegetation below easier targets on departure and approach, where it was common to see tracers zipping by the cockpit or rarely plunking the armor beneath the ejection seat at night. The airstrip was little more than a deathbed-in-waiting. It is conceivable that more flight crews perished operating around that field than in the heat of distant battles. Cannot confirm that bold statement, but scuttlebutt often had a way of being more believable than the sum of all official downloads.

With rumored air-conditioned quarters, well-furnished officers' clubs, level ten-thousand-foot concrete runways, and radar-equipped air traffic control often found in Air Force bases, the thing spoke for itself. That report of posh living was every bit scuttlebutt because Marines never received official invites to those Air Force clubs or living quarters in "country" nor free use of their local concrete runways. Instead, we Devil Dogs (As a Christian, I like to avoid that moniker), when faced with an emergency, a closed facility due to weather, or a fouled runway, were diverted to Air Force bases in Thailand, two countries away. Parenthetically, an Air Force pilot would only divert to our roller-coaster runway if in sheer distress and as a last resort.

Then, seeking a brief respite, a cup of java, and a little encouraging fellowship after his recent harrowing landing over a mechanical hangnail, a visit to "Bull Moose's" thatched roofed watering hole would only further shock the sensibilities of any temporarily detained Air Force officer trying to endure an already-bad hair day. Look, these airmen were accustomed to civilized life-sized paintings the likes of Robin Olds, their renowned Air Force ace, or other Air Force heroes emblazoned floor to ceiling on walls overlooking (so the story goes) fifty feet of spit-shined mahogany bars in full-service, air-conditioned restaurants. It is understandable that Air Force pilots were at a loss when denied those expectations as just one more annoyance when detained at our Marine Corps blue-collar air facility.

"Sounds like sour grapes to me, Marine," you say. Stay tuned, friend.

Truth was, like so many of my compadres, I loved roughing it. Why? Because I was a "can-do" Marine with a "can-do" attitude, which I was to learn—when left unchecked and managed without a little humility, a modicum of respect, and substantial help from our Commander in Chief, Jesus—can do you in. Consider the above a mere segue.

A Late-Night Fright Flight

On tonight's flight schedule there, I was slated for another ignominious middle-of-the-night TPQ hop to the DMZ, another boring, droning-on-and-on flight at twenty thousand feet to drop a small fortune of ordnance onto an intelligence officer's fantasy of what a true target might look like. The relentless wind and rain over the last days had temporarily subsided locally as we (to give my Skyhawk partner her just due) took the duty runway. After an uneventful carnival ride down the roller coaster, we made an end run around a small local weather system while climbing to altitude.

The little A-4E (only three or four feet longer but three thousand pounds lighter than our recently retired elderly class A Country Coach motorhome) was a valiant single-seat attack aircraft able to deliver nearly five tons of assorted ordinance and ascend to a service ceiling of over fifty thousand feet. The Skyhawk was also equipped with a standard pilot relief system for those with limited bladder capacity (a small rubber funnel attached to a hose disappearing to somewhere through the floor of the aircraft) but, mind you, with no weather radar to avoid thunderstorm cells which were, understandably, a primary reason you might need a relief tube. So, without weather radar, pilots used lightning flashes to slalom their way around thunderstorm cells.

Finding those cells this night was no more an issue than it was for World War II aviators with the same two eyes as ourselves. Eyeballing the plane around the cells to avoid lightning was a problem. Trying to avoid miles of monstrous South China Sea boomers while conquering their seventy-thousand-foot summits was pure fantasy. So, here was the lone strategy: avoid the main cells, ride out the bumps, take the lumps, drop the ordinance, and get back to bed.

Have you, like me, always been amazed at how reality can complicate strategy? Tonight would be a slalom by instrument flight in the "goo" all the way to Dong Ha. The ground radar technician in that facility bordering the South China Sea just south of the DMZ (oddly dubbed the "Demilitarized Zone" but alive with new North Vietnamese SAM III missiles) was already vectoring us to intercept tonight's final heading. The technician would remain in two-way-radio contact until the last ten seconds of our run; then, throughout that final interval, he would keep his transmitter keyed, denying an aviator any chance to audibly respond until we were bombs away.

During that brief period, the technician counted backward from ten, intending for us to release our ordinance over the target when he reached zero. Tonight, on final approach, he was closing us on an imposing "boomer." That was unsatisfactory. As the clouds became darker and denser and the air rougher, I radioed the controller twice about sending us into harm's way. No answers.

Following those failed transmissions, he began his countdown. Aborting the run would demand a change of course with a chance to avoid the thunderstorm; we had but eight seconds to make up our minds. The buck had, as usual, stopped in the cockpit; this dilemma needed a judgment call by yours truly. Aware of the Skyhawk's opinion, which she unwisely kept to herself, five more seconds and we would plunge into the edge of this nasty storm. "We can do this" was my "can-do" decision. No problem. Have I mentioned: "Can-do," Marine, "can do you in"?

A Haven of Enforced Humility

On zero (actually, I lost radio contact with the radar tech at two), I pickled (a military word to describe releasing ordinance . . . *and* tonight's "pickle" in which we were about to enter) the bombs in perfect unison with a blinding flash of lightning that pierced the darkness to the point, I presumed, of curling the Skyhawk's nose hairs but for certain ruining my night vision. Whoa, much too close! Then, unfolded the following sequence but not necessarily in its precise chronological order, in the blink of an eye, the aircraft, immersed in palpable ink, was bombarded by deafening fifty-caliber rounds of hail ricocheting off her fuselage and canopy. Brilliant florescent international green Saint Elmo's fire (an electrical discharge from the surrounding air)—outlining the fuel probe, bordering the windscreen, and lacing the cockpit—followed while the aircraft's pressure-driven instruments set to whirling like dervishes. Setting the power as recommended by the NATOPS flight manual for such an auspicious occasion, with eyes riveted on the artificial horizon to continue a straight and level flight, I held on for dear life. The ride had begun; not a serious rodeo fan, I rooted for this one to last less than eight seconds.

Up we went, and down we went. Up like a rocket, we zipped with positive G's, and down like a rock, we fell with negative G's. Positive G's following negative G's following positive G's following negative G's. Then came gushers and gushers of torrential rain (Wasn't I concerned this airborne tsunami was heavy enough to "flame out" my partner's engine?) while giant shards of lightning, crashing this side and that, would briefly illuminate the entire turbulent sky and cockpit like a thousand phosphorous flares to ruin what little night vision I had regained. Up and down went the altimeter's needle and rate of climb indicator, contradicting the true conditions of our actual flight. (I stopped scanning those instruments other than the artificial horizon and my radar altimeter designed to check in at four thousand feet above the ground.) Rocking and rolling, bumping and thumping, we pressed on and on into the eerie green of St. Elmo's hand. How long was this going to last anyway? Those eight seconds, I can tell you, were long gone with this cowboy still aboard the bronc. Should'a got a belt buckle for that rodeo ride.

Stories of aviators in parachutes spending over an hour in the clutches of these monsters came to mind. The commanding officer of my Meridian, Mississippi T-2 Buckeye Basic Jet training squadron, crinkled up like a broken pretzel following an ejection from an F-8 Crusader years earlier into a thunderstorm, was reminder enough of my wish not to leave the relative comfort of this uncomfortable carnival ride. Would the result be the same for us as for that commander, or could we ride this out? Could we get out at all? I did not know and was too busy to think about it and too busy helping the little aircraft stay wings-level so she could do her job. If we survived, I would have to apologize and thank my little flying friend. At least I had been out of the weather.

Then, presto, instant deliverance. Spewed forth into smooth air and under a full moon at eleven o'clock high, my radar altimeter had kicked in, showing our altitude to be a little less than four thousand feet above ground after losing sixteen-thousand feet, all the while maintaining a level flight attitude. We had been no more than that monster's temporary dalliance until it spit us out. Nothing foreign to a thunderstorm belongs anywhere near one, my friend.

Gratefully, below us, outlined in the shadows of a brilliant moon, lay the DMZ exactly where it belonged but clearly where we didn't. Then, with gratitude waning, I wondered if those SAM III ground-to-air missiles closeted among the shadows below were night fliers? Did not know. Man, oh man, from the frying pan into the fire.

No Room at the Inn

Staying beneath an overcast and swinging south, we ran into another wall of lightning, which forced us seaward into a climb and, I might add, that well-known fantasy of surmounting a South China Sea boomer. Avoiding the cells, we reached the aircraft's fifty-two thousand feet of service ceiling with ample proof no one outclimbs a South China Sea thunderstorm. The Skyhawk was uncomfortably trying to keep her balance but slipping and sliding in the thin air at that altitude; she did not like it much, nor was she alone. Something else for which to seek an apology.

After our recent unstable, not-so-much-of-a-joyride, I had hoped to keep our distance from any cells on our return to base; regrettably, there was no choice but to confront them again. Descending while swinging further south, Scooter and I negotiated our way, one at a time, around every lighted cell. Approaching the field while still in zero visibility "goo," the runway duty officer relayed Chu Lai's strip was socked in by weather, a disappointment but no major surprise on this unsettled night. Using the radar altimeter (which, again, accurately gives altitude in feet above the ground), I eased down to fifty of those feet and used the faint glow from the runway duty officers' shack through the opaque cloud cover to estimate the runway's position.

Due to tonight's unintentionally extended flight time, my bingo fuel of a little over twelve hundred pounds (the predetermined quantity needed to reach our alternate field in Thailand) would let us squeeze in but two passes at Chu Lai. Neither gave me a visual of the runway, so I raised the gear and flaps and began our climb due west on the 270-degree radial. The fuel load required was based on a clean aircraft, one configured without wing tanks. Pulling the handle to jettison both, the left tank remained tenaciously attached to the Skyhawk. That was not good, not at all good. The extra parasite drag from that hanging tank would cost extra fuel, and I was already pushing eleven hundred pounds. Looking back, should I have made but one pass in Chu Lai? Poor headwork? Wrong choice? Time would tell. Spilt milk. "Can-do," Marine, can do you in!

The call sign for the controlling authority in Thailand was "lion," which I transmitted until hoarse without success over the guard channel (an emergency radio channel monitored by all facilities and aircraft within range). Climbing to altitude (and at last into an uncloudy sky) where jet engines are most efficient, I adjusted the Skyhawk's power to gain as many miles per pound of fuel as possible. Successive attempts to chain off that hitchhiker under our left wing, calling "lion" with reckless abandon, and trying to conserve fuel were all proving futile. Whoa, I was getting a tad tense. While considering our least desirable outcome—running the main fuel tank dry followed by an ejection (which I deliberately withheld from Scooter)—the Ubon RTAB (Royal Thai Air Base) navigational aid jumped online to confirm our heading to be on the money. At least one thing was going right. "Lion" came up ten minutes before our scheduled arrival, tracked the approach, and handed us off to a US Air Force controller (having graciously bathed the field ahead with light), who approved a straight-in precision approach but only after we had declared an emergency fuel state. I will say: A fuel gauge needle tickling "Empty" at five thousand feet is a moment to remember.

Were the aircraft's tank to run dry, I was high and fast approaching the numbers (the near end of the runway) to give us a little cushion.

The landing was routine, although a little further down that beautiful ten thousand feet of concrete than usual. Remember that any landing an aviator and his charge walk away from at such times qualifies as a good landing.

In the Lap of Luxury

Scooter and I were greeted at the far end of that exquisite runway by a "follow-me" vehicle that ushered us to the flight line and "visitor's parking." Really? Visitor's parking? Really! After completing the yellow maintenance sheet and specifying the fuel load for the morning, the follow-me drove this relieved pilot to an all-night restaurant at the officers' club. An all-night restaurant? Really? Really! Entering the lobby, I faced what could have been the longest mahogany bar in history. Multiple squadron photographs dotted the walls, but over the bar proper hung a bigger-than-life-sized portrait of handlebar-mustachioed Colonel Robin Olds, the highly decorated Air Force ace. (Remember? As prophesied.) Surveying my surroundings, I felt a little like an Untouchable at a Brahman banquet. Whoa, wasn't this a civilized notch or two above Bull Moose's Mega Hut in Chu Lai. After devouring a gourmet meal and dessert, a taxi (that is right, a real taxi!) dropped me at a private air-conditioned apartment (What?!) to remain overnight. Only briefly did I mull over an inter-service transfer during that night's slumber and early morning's hottest of showers.

During dawn's pre-flight, the line crew informed this Marine there remained but seventy-five pounds (about nine gallons and less than 1 percent of our original fuel load) in his Skyhawk's tank at last night's shutdown. That amount of fuel, I was told, would not have been enough to get us through the downwind leg had a go-around been necessary last night. The decisions to challenge that thunderstorm over Dong Ha, to surmount and avoid the weather on the way back to Chu Lai, the second attempt to land there, and the malfunction that prevented the jettison of the left wing's fuel tank, taken together, illustrate how so many aircraft accidents occur when one small, less-than-ideal decision or incident is followed by others. (I decided not to share that fact with my faithful little Skyhawk; trust issues loom large in aviation, folks.)

Then, off we asymmetrically limped, one hanging tank and all, back to "hooch haven," the inevitable stack of paperwork waiting at my "real job" as the squadron's administrative officer, and to my relief, never a question as to why I was tardy for work. I chose not to talk about it, anyway. Incidentally, there was nary a cloud in the sky. Checking the flight schedule, I had two hops. Wonderful day to be alive as an aviator! A blessed "twofer."

All's Well That Ends Well

Could any Marine be more impressed or conflicted by that luxurious Air Force base? Yet, after hearing the daily losses sustained by those F-105 Thunderchief drivers, who flew with Colonel Olds to encounter MIGS, SAM missiles, and anti-aircraft flack over the north, my esteem for Air Force aviation surged in a heartbeat; those aviators deserved every amenity and more they were given. Funny how our feet can suddenly find trouble filling other people's shoes, isn't it? And last night? Well, it was another Spartan-Athenian experience. Here I was, a Spartan without so much as a seeing-eye dog to help me land in zero visibility on an unlighted roller coaster at Chu Lai, only to escape to an Athenian base at Ubon offering a precision radar approach to ten thousand feet of emblazoned runway under a full moon and unlimited visibility. Now add a "follow-me" guide to the "visitor's" flight line, a gourmet dinner, and, unbelievably, private air-conditioned sleeping quarters. Something did not compute. How did I end up on this side of such an outrageously unbalanced world of military aviation, anyway?

"Probably the same way you waffled your way into that humungous thunderstorm over the DMZ, tried to create your own Tower of Babel on the way back, took one too many rides around that invisible merry-go-round in Chu Lai and, surprise of surprises, put us into an emergency fuel state while running on fumes to Thailand last night. That can-do attitude, you know, can do us both in, Marine. Do you need to hear that again?" my tired, beat up, pockmarked, hypothermic, thirsty little Skyhawk with a hanging wing tank might have voiced had she enough energy to volunteer her opinion over the whole near miss of a mess. That run-on sentence was not nearly as long as that night's circus, pardner.

Might I have responded to that snarky little bird by questioning why she refused to let loose that wing tank? Perhaps, had I been prone to hold a conversation with an aircraft.

Postscript

A handful of factors, which must include communication equipment failures (in the guts of a bombing run, for example), mechanical mishaps (say, a stuck wing tank), or inclement weather systems (maybe multiple monster thunderstorms or a socked-in home base) are occasionally unavoidable in military aviation; most parts of a routine flight, however, are under a pilot's control. So, a split second late, an ounce of fuel wasted, a knot of airspeed lost, a foot of runway behind or a foot of altitude above (all under control of the pilot) are among solitary or cumulative factors incriminated in accident causation.

Had we avoided those red flags that night? Few, if any. Yet there we were, that little Skyhawk and her driver, "fat, dumb, and happy" again, not only having hobbled around all last night's "bases" but, wonder of wonders, now celebrating a grand slam. So, let us get real: That night's outcome, chock full of those "solitary and cumulative factors" incriminated in past pilots' "buying the farm," had instead turned into an unforgettable Michael Jordan buzzer beater, once-in-a-lifetime Doug Flutie Hail Mary pass, unapproachable Hank Aaron record-setting home run, and one more unmerited, undeserved, and unearned Kiss from Heaven. Whoa, how does that happen? Who can turn an eleventh-hour nightmare, where we clung as the last drop from the pointy end of an entire funnel's worth of poor headwork, into a dream come true?

If you have yet to figure that one out, wisdom would be for you to introduce yourself to Jesus, appropriately named our Savior. You might begin with gratitude for His having made all your past self-engineered potential disasters into near misses. Remember those events confidently assigned by you as "dumb luck," "bacon-saving karma," or "beating the odds" after serial bad decisions you "got away with"? Truth is, God sent His Son as a Savior because we needed a Savior that none should perish (John 3:16) and then Holy Spirit as a Helper because we needed help (John 14:26). We always will. So, let me share another not-so-well-guarded Kiss from Heaven: Wise men (and wise pilots) still seek Him (and the other Him, too).

QUESTION: Where is the Kiss from Heaven from this God Story?

ANSWER: How large of a container will seventy-five pounds (about nine gallons) of JP-4 jet fuel fill? Well, how about less than two small barbeque-sized propane tanks, two five-gallon gas cans for your mower, a beginner's aquarium, a stackable ten-gallon storage tote . . . and the beat goes on. Hard to tell how far that nine gallons of JP-4 in the Scooter would have carried us that night if a wave-off and repeat approach had been necessary. Be certain, however, that Vegas would not have touched such a wager. Of one thing we may be assured: Had we tried a third roundabout in Chu Lai, I would have missed a great gourmet supper and an outstanding night's sleep in Ubon. I'm not sure about you, but I must dub the final act of that cliffhanger a Kiss from Heaven with our brave little pockmarked Scooter adding her "Amen."

The Crow Convention (1972)

What caught my eye through the cabin's window was a young crow lighting upon a lower branch of a large snow-encrusted hemlock about twenty feet downhill from the cabin. We were midway through Central New York's winter of 1972 when Gretel, our family's German shorthaired pointer, and I holed up for a frosty week in the family's summer cottage on now-frozen Skaneateles Lake. I focused on reviewing the last four years of my medical studies to prepare for upcoming board exams, while the dog, in character, was overwhelmingly more focused on catching up on her sleep. On that bitter, frigid day, the blustery winds were giving most windowpanes in our elderly cabin an ongoing case of the rattles and giving the dog, uncomfortably curled into a shivering donut on an overstuffed chair in a corner of the room, an equally responsive ongoing case of the growls. Rattle, growl, rattle, growl—you get the drift.

It was not long before those industrious howling winds had swept the entire frozen surface of the lake in front of the cabin clear of snow while, regrettably, forgetting to remove another two feet of the white stuff obscuring everything else in sight and keeping me cabin-bound with all those rattles, growls, and howls. I grumbled about getting little done amidst all the bedlam, took a break, and shifted my gaze to the only short-term distraction available, the young crow perched upon that hemlock limb downhill to the east.

What soon peaked and focused my full attention was a steadily mounting influx of similar young sentinel crows assembling in skeletonized trees bordering both a gurgling creek on one side of the cabin and a snow-covered footpath on the other, each ambling its way downhill toward the lake. Seamlessly, a progressive number of more mature crows trailing their younger sentinel predecessors then swooped in from the west over the peak of our building to settle on the snow-covered beach and frozen shallows. As if an afterthought, a handful of larger and clearly more aged birds followed, slipping in among the rest. Within seconds, a swelling cacophony of cawing from the growing crow population penetrated my already-porous single-pane windows overlooking the entire event. The decibel levels rose sharply when two more flights landed in a comparable way to the first, one from the northeast followed by another from the southeast. Unmitigated chaos and unrelenting din suddenly took over my world.

Mesmerized, I cautiously withdrew into a more dimly lit area of the room to preserve my anonymity from the wary avian sentinels perched among the surrounding trees and, by then, about two hundred birds weaving themselves enthusiastically, harmoniously, and noisily into a single giant living, pulsating, black, fun-loving orb on the ice. It is impossible not to say this: For the next twenty or more minutes, it was a time set aside to meet, greet, socialize, and "party" with abandon.

Then, without warning or obvious instruction, the celebratory orb morphed within heartbeats into an imposing black donut, a hole ten to fifteen feet in diameter quickly commanding its center. That move alone was artistically synchronized as if lifted from a professionally choreographed Broadway production. It was a crisp and instantaneous scene change, a reset tinged with a sense of anticipation, purpose, and gravitas, which instantly dampened its own cacophony.

Gradually but intentionally, contingents of three or four large elderly crows exited from spaces occupied in the orb by their respective flocks to enter that "donut hole." At their entrance, the decibel level fell precipitously to near zero. Then, each "elder" intentionally and successively approached each of the other "elders," one bird at a time. The birds met within the circle, a smaller ring of crows, rotating it seemed within a larger one, methodically bobbing their heads in repetitive face-to-face encounters. The separate encounters lasted a minute or more (in what I presumed to be communication) before moving along to the next crow. It appeared as if the intended goal for each "leader" was to "reach out" and "converse" with every other "leader" of the "council" before the "meeting" was over. I estimate this ritual continued for twenty minutes or longer. During this interval, the entire periphery of younger crows, in what I presumed to be a sign of deference and respect, waited patiently and in near but not perfect silence, holding their places and their tongues. (As you can see, it has always been hard to tell this tale without assigning anthropomorphic motives to the birds. I would like to leave that to science and the ornithologists, impossible as that would be.)

Again, without warning, although the crows did not appear the least bit surprised, the elderly leaders eased out of the inner circle (donut hole) in force and melted back among their respective families on the ice. Then, the donut hole vanished as quickly as it had formed, the orb in its entirety reappeared, and, like a huge blackberry pie cut into thirds, the birds separated themselves by three feet of space into three groups. In reverse order of their earlier arrivals, the flocks ("murders" for serious crow folks) took flight, starting with the one from the southeast, followed by the northeast contingent and ending with the remaining birds who disappeared over the cabin to the west. The sentinels, all provided by the western flock (as far as I could tell), continued their respective watches until the final flight had vacated the beach area. Then, one after the other, those birds skimmed the peak of our roof in pursuit of the main body until but one lone youngster, occupying that snow-crusted hemlock branch about twenty feet down the hill, abandoned his duty station and vanished from sight.

Talk About Afterglow

What an incredible, uniquely orchestrated private spectacular had played out before my unabashedly spying eyes. Curiously, I do recall feeling strangely uncomfortable thereafter, a little guilty, as if I had crashed a wedding ceremony. Look, I had been an uninvited and undiscovered interloper to a big-time clan meeting, a carefully arranged and executed and intentionally secret generational gathering of crows from differing points on the compass. There had been new members to meet, old relationships to strengthen, news to share, and business to conduct. It had been a time for socializing and fun and a time for diplomacy and gravitas. Who says you cannot mix business with pleasure? Was it a routine affair or an emergency get-together? Who knows? What I came to understand that day was this: Crows, who I had always admired for their sense of community and intelligence, had taken both to a whole new level.

I looked again at the slew of medical books about the table. Despite being intimately familiar with these tomes—culminations of centuries of professional thought, learning, and investigation by brilliant academics, researchers, and practitioners—I was feeling a little less near the top of the planet's intellectual food chain and not so savvy as I had been an hour ago. I recall wondering if there were other species out there in the animal kingdom who were as organized, disciplined, and congenial as those crows and as successfully secretive about it.

Then, I caught the green-eyed Gretel dog, now alert and squinting at me from that big easy chair in the corner. It was as if she was trying to decide whether those sacred crow rites had somehow been compromised. When I looked again, to no surprise, the dog had resumed her nap, after concluding, I assumed, the crows' secret remained safe for another eon. Gretel never had a whole lot of respect for human intelligence, particularly mine. With that less-than-bolstering thought, merely another slice from that day's humble pie, I felt more motivated than ever to burn some midnight oil.

Postscript

Ponder this: When have we ever been privy to a three-hundred-member meeting, conference, or legislative session conducted between three equivalent groups that concluded business in less than an hour? Never, correct? So, here is a question: Why are we humans, with the highest intelligence quotients on the planet, eternally in gridlock from school boards to Congress to Baptist landscaping committees squabbling over which color tulip to plant outside the narthex? Why are we unable to start and conclude our business with the congeniality and dispatch of a crow gathering without it landsliding into an agonizing Phineas T. Bluster media extravaganza that lasts longer than the meeting itself? That could only occur by demanding solemn respect for the system, the process, and the other participants.

The elders in our crow convention seemed genuinely intent on concluding their business but never at the expense of established protocols or relationships. Purpose and respect reigned, while resistance and contempt were excluded from the process. So, why would the Lord give "lower" animals such "higher" skills and leave us humans languishing? Then I remembered Adam's fall and had to conclude that, seeing the handwriting on the wall, the crows in Eden, determined not to become collateral damage when things unraveled, were long gone to Maui before the whole apple-eating debacle unfolded, the gig in the garden was canceled, and everybody was asked to leave the hood. That revelation made considerable sense to this man.

QUESTION: Where is the Kiss from Heaven in this God Story?

ANSWER: After considerable research, the ornithological literature I reviewed lacked a single recording of an entire crow convention, the likes of which I had witnessed. What a privilege to see those birds conduct such a civilized, respectful, and successful event. Then, I realized Jesus was the crows' Creator too. That gave me a dash of hope we humans might yet again find our way. Those birds, it seemed, never lost theirs. Later, I discovered crows find apples (their seeds, like those of the pomegranate, are laced with the poison cyanide) way down the bird's list of known culinary delights (eggs, meat, vegetables, berries, unsalted nuts, grains, and other seeds), which cause them to avoid both those infamous fruits and likely prompted their rapid departure from the garden. Too bad Eve didn't get that message in advance; you are aware we humans and cyanide aren't exactly bedfellows either.

We might be left with a question about medicine's long-entrenched health axiom, "An apple a day keeps the doctor away." Relax, Christian, no need to fear for the apple's honored place as a healthy human food. After a survey of 40,000 women eating one apple per day, scientists found a 13 to 22 percent reduction in cardiovascular risk,[1] strongly suggesting from that study that crows and humans have much more in common with Maui than with apples.

---

[1] Jeanelle Boyer & Rui Hai Liu, "Apple Phytochemicals and Their Health Benefits," *Nutrition Journal* vol 3, no. 5, https://nutritionj.biomedcentral.com/articles/10.1186/1475-2891-3-5.

Master Repairman (1974)

Elmer had a carrot top with an Elvis "doo," stood well beyond six foot two, not counting the hair, and spoke with a voice like a lullaby. Women, after meeting him, said that he was "sweet," and men, given the same opportunity, could not help admitting he was a "really good guy." His looks and demeanor, however, effectively betrayed his history as a hardened veteran of Mission Aviation Fellowship (MAF), a missionary bush pilot who had flown herkie, supply-laden, single-engine Cessna 206s (as I recall) in and out of severely remote South American mountain jungle airstrips for years.

Landing upon those mountainside runways, often climbing like roller coasters on final approach, demanded every inch of throttle on touch down if Elmer's plane were to claw its way up the next three hundred feet to the far end of an airstrip. Then, punching a brake to snap turn the bird 180 degrees into a position, local natives would spring into action. A handful would strain to hold the tail back and down while others dove beneath the bird, feverishly throwing chocks in front of its two impatient wheels. They worked determinedly to deny the plane any chance at a premature downhill trip leading to a precipice perched thousands of feet above an unwary valley floor, lounging below in a false sense of security.

Only aviators could fathom what Elmer did for a living, while even fewer recognized his commitment, grasped his courage, and understood his level of skill. After tonight's slide show, I thought the church would hold a much greater appreciation for this very John Wayne-like hero.

Well, maybe or not. Elmer, Brother Mac, our pastor, and I had been working for over an hour to hook up the night's audiovisual equipment. The 1970s-style Kodak slide projector was reluctant to function from the outset. Elmer had stripped the machine to a skeleton to rebuild it at least twice within an hour. The results? It remained dead in the water. Mac and I offered occasional unsolicited suggestions to which Elmer gave rapt attention, full consideration, and sincere appreciation despite how inane. He was simply a kind and respectful Christian gentleman. Rapidly approaching our 6:00 p.m. start, with hopes fading to resurrect the projector, we finally surrendered to destiny while standing zombie-like, shrugging our shoulders in unison, and staring at each other like the three stooges. Trying to energize the carousel tray (prehistoric equipment for you PowerPoint and beyond people) with the handheld remote had disappointed us for the umpteenth time when suddenly Brother Mac suggested, "Why don't we pray?"

Why do I so vividly recall this moment? Maybe because my silence and self-restraint contradicted the forthright stance I take on most things. As a newer Christian, I felt embarrassed, a little repulsed, and curiously irritated. The whole prayer thing was a little too over the top for me. Come on, Pastor, asking God to show up like a heavenly Maytag repairman, bow tie and all, to fix a slide projector, and that on a Sunday evening seemed in my eyes to severely diminish the stature of the King of Kings and Lord of Lords. And what about the whole Sabbath rest thing?

While I wrestled with contradictions, Brother Mac was wrestling with Jesus: "Lord, sorry we didn't ask for your help sooner. We know you want us to depend upon you. Please forgive us. You know all things, and nothing is too hard for you. Lord, we have but moments until the service starts; please repair our projector. Thank you, Jesus. In your name, we pray, Amen."

Elmer and I added our "Amens" in unison; for me, it was a perfunctory response.

Not only did I not appreciate this weird religious stuff, but I also believed nothing would come from it. God, the repairman? *Gimme a break, guys*, I thought, *get real*. Elmer, however, depended on prayer routinely on the mission field where life in a troubled cockpit often became as real as it gets. And Mac was a praying pastor, as he (although belatedly) showed tonight. For those two, God the repairman? Most certainly! So, they, unlike myself, had remained expectant. Then, Elmer casually flipped the power switch for the umpteenth attempt plus one, which instantly lit up the screen like a Hollywood spectacular as the slides fed into the machine with ease. Everything was a definite "go." Mac and Elmer thanked the Lord with abundant sincerity while I stood dumbfounded, my mouth nicely simulating a gaping black hole in space.

Could it be that I was wrong, or was this a coincidence? Was God willing to tend to this minutia when so many of humanity's glaring needs lay unfulfilled at His feet? Mac laughingly challenged those thoughts: "God was just waiting around for us to ask."

Oh my, I found it even harder to believe that outlandish statement. Really? God was waiting around. Like, with nothing to do? Let us just say that I ended with more questions than answers, which I tucked away in the busyness of the moment for another time. And for sure, this was not it.

Instead, we had Elmer's slideshow to watch, which, incidentally, was way beyond the ordinary and deservedly forged his "hero's" reputation among the church that night in hardened steel.

A Lawnmower in Need

Oregon became a veritable patchwork quilt of green every spring, especially when the Willamette Valley grass seed fields were growing in "fast forward." Fortunately for us, our home was situated to the south of that variegated valley and sheltered from its constant maze of chartreuse pollen-laden clouds that roamed its fields as reckless mobs, often mandating panic-laced avoidance maneuvers by any car carrying an asthmatic.

Ours was a secluded homestead, sequestered on a crewcut summit surrounded by imposing old-growth Douglas firs from whose heights echoed screeching self-righteous ospreys and equally vain eagles, eternally squabbling over fishing rights in the waters below. Before us to the north, diamond studded in any midday sun, stretched Dorena Reservoir in her five miles of mountain-cradled magnificence. Christened years before when a small town deriving its name from two inseparable local friends, Dora Barnette and Rena Martin (I am merely reporting history here), was intentionally submerged beneath the reservoir's dark waters as part of a massive flood control project. This time of year, the evening skies above our reservoir became a rapidly changing kaleidoscope of colors and hues, often enhanced by velvet mists issuing from the indigo waters below. This morning, however, the only color that captivated me was the suffused green of my out-of-control lawn, which had obscured all sprinkler heads, baseball mitts, and my best pair of hedge trimmers. The grass needed mowing and needed it now.

I rarely played hooky from church, but Sunday was the only day left from this weekend. Despite the success of Saturday's marathon family work party, I still had an acre of grass to mow and a forest of weeds to, well, weed. Within scant minutes after the family had left for Sunday school, the lawnmower quit. Soon, with the disabled machine disassembled on the garage floor, I actively searched out the reason for the sudden engine seizure. Fortunately, the problem was diagnosable and corrective action a breeze. Feeling good about the progress, I was confident that within minutes, mowing would begin again. Finishing, I began to self-talk, "Four bolts to secure, and we are finished . . . now three . . . now, two . . . and finally, one left. Wait a minute, what is going on? Those four bolts are all the same gauge and length. Yet this last one is not taking hold of anything. No purchase at all! Let me look at the threads. No, the threads are fine. Let me try one of the other bolts. OK, remove this one and try it where the last one could gain no purchase . . . no luck. Union stripped? Highly unlikely. This makes no sense. OK, let me try the other two bolts. Is there something peculiar to one of them? Nope, not that one. Nuts, this other one does not work either. This is getting a bit frustrating, let alone time-consuming."

Then, without warning, the whole scene from the long-forgotten church slideshow flooded my mind. It was impossible not to smile as I mused over that earlier time. A major national news program had recently interviewed Elmer flying supplies to starving refugees in Ethiopia. Brother Mac, I knew, was working in a senior's ministry for a megachurch near Fullerton, California. Escaping my reverie, this present situation had all the earmarks of that earlier one. Having tried repeatedly and unsuccessfully to seat that bolt deep in the recess from where it came, I had come to the end of my rope. No answers were forthcoming. This day's problem mimicked that past debacle.

Without hesitation but still struggling with what seemed the intellectual nonsense of it all, I dusted off Mac's old prayer as I remembered it: "Lord, forgive me for not asking sooner. This lawnmower appears unfixable. Mac said you want us to depend on you, and I know that you know what is wrong with this machine. So, Lord, could you show me how to repair it or even fix it yourself? Jesus, I would really appreciate it. In your name, I pray. Amen." Well, that was that.

"Okay. Here is the bolt. Into the hole with you, my friend," I sighed. "Now, a clockwise turn and, whoa—thank you, Jesus! Thank you, Lord! It worked; it tightened down!"

How often had I tried to seat that bolt, or one like it, before praying? Well, at least a dozen times. To this day, I know not what happened in the deep recesses of that dark little orifice. All I understood was this: I prayed, and the bolt stayed. That was enough to clear those lingering doubts I had carried over the last ten years about praying over inanimate objects. I pondered why the Lord chose that morning to seal such a practical lesson in my memory bank. Did He orchestrate that scenario to effectively build my faith by experiencing answered prayer, or, as I long ago believed, did He want me to know that, although I missed church that morning, I was not to miss my Sunday school lesson?

An End-Stage Toyota

There are the best of times and the worst of times. But of all the times for car problems to raise their ugly head, on that day, they reached the pinnacle of all inconvenience. In unsolicited divorce proceedings, I had but little liquidity and was traveling sixty miles one way to work and back five days a week and living in the tiny back bedroom of a merciful Christian brother's home. And now, without warning, here comes this infernal racket, the kind that resonates from heavy metal grinding heavy metal coming from the deepest recesses of my Toyota pickup's bell housing. To make things worse, it was getting louder and louder as the days went by. The truck deserved a mechanic, but I had only a gas credit card, my checking account was empty, and the next paycheck was two weeks away. That evening, on my way "home" from work, I was trying to somehow disregard the heightening cacophony beneath my feet while, among everything else that was happening, wondering how I would manage this latest insult.

Life had become a watershed for one disaster after another, with no flood relief in sight. Exiting the freeway, the dissenting bell housing swiveled pedestrians' heads down the entirety of Main Street. By the time I reached the house, the din was deafening. There was no way

I could drive this vehicle 120 miles tomorrow. What an unmitigated nightmare! Besides, I knew no one whose work was anywhere near my own. Turning off the ignition key, I paused, needing a moment of peace, artificial as it might be. Once again, my mind jolted back to the church in Southern California and to Elmer's stalled slideshow. Then it flashed to the garage on Dorena Lake where no bolt could find purchase in the recesses of that disabled lawnmower.

Evaluating the possibilities without a grain of faith did not help. In the depths of my recent troubles, my heart had become so cold, hard, and dry. Well, at least I could not be deceived by any errant feelings of false faith when I had few feelings at all. Small comfort. Still, I had one thing, a history, a record of documented successes using prayer to bring about "restoration" or, at the minimum, "repair" of failed inanimate objects. What had I to lose?

Offering one quick prayer, I would then whisk into the house for supper. Laying my hand on the dashboard with sudden emotion I thought unavailable, I prayed along these lines: "Jesus, you are the same yesterday, today, and forever. So, I should have come to you earlier, Lord. You remember repairing the projector and the lawnmower, don't you? Well, I have another favor to ask. Without transportation, I cannot make it to work tomorrow. Lord, you know what is wrong with this truck, but I surely do not. All I know is that it sounds serious. Lord, would you fix it for me? In your name. Amen."

Removing my hand from the dashboard, I opened the door, entered the house, ate a fine meal, went to bed, forgot about the truck, and never once thought to arrange transportation to work the next morning.

Following breakfast, I hustled from my friend's home with little time to spare, jumped into the "disabled" truck, and started the engine. Quickly reminded of yesterday's predicament, realized that the old girl, after a preceding week of progressively increasing complaints from her bell housing, was purring like a kitten.

Not as surprised this time but ecstatic beyond reason, I could not be quiet the rest of the week about my miracle. People gathered about in droves at work to hear the testimony. There were those who cried, while more laughed. Others praised Jesus. Others thought I had lost it. Then, there were those who could not care less. Well, Christian, neither did I. Hey, I had my ride back, I had my testimony, and Jesus got the glory. Who could ask for anything more?

Somewhere around 200,000 miles and years later, I bargained away the old Toyota for my second son's motorcycle to get him off the highway so I could get a little sleep. He gleaned over a half-dozen more years from that truck's still-reliable drive train before he sold her to another fortunate soul. That the trusty Toyota is still cruising around the USA with a satisfied owner behind the wheel would be no surprise. After all, she had been touched by the Master Repairman.

A CD Mystery

Mordecai was our 1995 Monaco Windsor coach, a thirty-three-foot beauty with a beefed-up 230 HP Cummins diesel, who towed Ester, our 1994 Saturn four-door sedan. (Do you, like us, give names to your vehicles?) Together, the five of us, Mordecai, Ester, Emily, Daisy dog, and I, followed the Lord around the USA for about seven years. Living in an RV is a true test of a marriage, and when we finally returned to a stick-built home, we knew we had passed the test. It was a glorious seven years full of adventure, romance, intrigue, and danger.

For example, have you ever done a "wheelie" in a thirty-three-foot RV? It is something you do not want to try at home, friend. How about backing up Friday evening rush-hour traffic on the downtown Dallas 183 freeway for five miles to change a fuel filter? You can bet we will never win an election in Big "D." What about getting stuck in mud so deep it takes two giant tow trucks to extract you? That move will never endear you as a member of the Good Sam Club. Have you ever left your rig for two weeks in the Texas summer sun only to have your failed freezer full of pot roast thaw during your absence? Not an olfactory delight for months and months and months. How about inadvertently depositing a spill of "blue water" ten feet in diameter on the icy parking lot outside your motel room during an Upstate New York winter? It takes more snow than you can imagine concealing a blue orb that big.

Then, there we were, wearily waiting after six hours in stalled traffic for an accident to clear the freeway in Nebraska, only to hear a deep Southern trucker's drawl cheerily boom forth from our CB radio, "While I'm a-waitin', ah think I'll fetch a bucket and wash ma truck." Laughed so hard I needed the restroom. Fortunately, we had one. Have you ever heard scores and scores of truckers laugh over a CB radio? It can make a long day a little shorter. How about spending two hours spread-eagle against a wall, frisked, and then detained while your rig was torn end to end by Canadian border patrol agents after they found three rounds to a weapon long before banished from the RV? When Canada says no weapons, they mean it, sir.

Now, Mordecai had given us seventy or eighty thousand good miles and remained mechanically sound except for periodic replacement of worn parts and routine maintenance. There was one irreparable problem, however. Somewhere along our journey, the rig's CD player, which had functioned as advertised for the first four years, had given up the ghost. After taking the dash apart and checking all the electrical connections, fuses, and anything else that came to mind, I considered it a lost cause. (The company would fix it if I came to Indiana. Let us not go there now, and we did not go there then.) For three years thereafter, however, we traveled with a portable CD player sitting on the couch behind Emily's passenger's chair. It was a pragmatic solution.

Toward our long journey's end, we settled in Port Isabel, Texas, and bought a park model with a room added on in Long Island Village, a quasi-retirement community along the Intracoastal Waterway. It was time to rest Mordecai, so we had him consigned to a recreational vehicle dealership just south of Fort Worth. It would take us over ten hours to complete the trip north after carefully detailing our faithful friend.

True to our calculations, ten hours after leaving home, we were five miles south of our destination when a thought about the rig's CD player, a significant source of aggravation over the last three years, crossed my mind. Now, nearing the conclusion of our journey and for the first time, I sensed that the Lord wanted us to pray over that broken machine. *Really, Lord,* I thought, *do you really want to repair it?*

What then came to mind was the projector, then the lawnmower, and finally the Toyota. Was Jesus about to do another miracle? "OK, Lord," I said, "we will pray."

Sharing with Emily what I thought was going on in Heaven, we prayed, laying hands upon the controls of that intractable would-be music maker: "Lord," we asked, "you know what's wrong with this CD player. Would you repair it for us so the rig will sell and the next folks will have a blessing? In Jesus' name, we pray."

Emily rushed to insert a CD, and music filled the air. *Oh, Lord, you have done it again.* I thought, *I can't . . . uh, well, of course, I can believe it. Thank you so much, Lord, for your concern, especially for the things we leave in the care of others. How gracious you are.*

Postscript

If the Lord is so receptive to prayers for audiovisual equipment malfunction, small engine breakdown, automotive drive train difficulty, and CD player failure, then I would think that the Bible would be replete where God fixed broken stuff for His people. There may be isolated incidents; if so, I long ago forgot any in the Scriptures. Could it be that God did not get interested until He discovered that humanity was not so easily fixable? If we consider the Lord's success with humankind, from Adam to Moses to the law to the judges to the kings to the prophets to the cross and to the Spirit, we humans leave abundant room for improvement, wouldn't you say? For someone good at fixing mechanical stuff, why has Father had such limited success with people?

Deep inside, we all know at least one of the primary reasons: Inanimate stuff does not have a choice, but humans do; we can resist. Do you know that the most common reason the hearts of God's people never find healing? That is right—because people refuse. Now, I am not talking about coronary artery disease, congestive heart failure, or valvular heart disease, but I refer to the spiritually and emotionally brokenhearted of His kingdom. Truly, the hearts of God's people are so often sick, wounded, neglected, abused, needy, deceived, or sinful that one might expect all of humanity lined up eight across and nations deep for help. But no, that is not the case, is it? Why are we Christians more than willing to spend time in prayer to repair a carousel of slides, mow a lawn, drive a car, or listen to a bunch of tunes than to spend a New York minute on the abuse, neglect, torment, or depraved conditions of our own hearts?

Since you asked, here is the plain vanilla for healing our hearts' inner pain. At first, we Homo sapiens often defy any accountability to God or man by championing our own solutions birthed in belief systems often founded on lies we embrace as truth; then, we complicate our distress by using pain management choices, which themselves generate even more pain.

Look, here is a fact: What you believe you will feel, what you believe and feel you will act out, and what you believe, feel, and act out will cause consequences, good or bad. All of us regrettably hold our own beliefs to be impeccably true, try to live by them honestly, and then, without a moment's consideration, they may be inaccurate and ourselves deceived by adhering to them, stubbornly attribute the damages of our own actions to others' behavior. By any other name, we will still blame others for our own stuff.

Here is the problem: It is easier to manage our aberrant belief systems and the hurtful behaviors arising from them by defending ourselves, blaming others, numbing ourselves to their consequences, or performing our ways out of those consequences than to expose honestly and willingly our pain-laced, tainted, and error-laden belief systems to which we adhere and follow as truth. The fact is that we are reluctant to a fault to admit our deception, enter extended work with Holy Spirit to renew our minds with truth (Rom.12:2), come into belief systems that line up with God's Word, and be set free from the painful consequences of our lie-based thinking. (Will you please ponder that penetrating, universal truth for a moment?)

This is worth repeating: As humans, we would rather exercise our God-given free will by declining to have any of our emotional Achilles' heels exposed, painful lie-producing memories explored, and fallacies in our thinking discovered by simply hiding them under our fig leaves of simple psychological defenses, numbing mechanisms, and culturally accepted performance-based ways to lie to ourselves. Unfortunately, we humans also routinely resist Holy Spirit's advances and refuse to honestly open ourselves to His ministry. Rather, we prefer to choose our own course while our Comforter, Counselor, Helper, Strengthener, Teacher, Guide, Intercessor, Advocate, and Friend looks on. Sadly, it is not enough this resistance leads us to become stunted Christians but that the outcome tragically trickles down to negatively affect our loved ones, friends, churches, communities, and, if we can see the big picture over time, the potential entirety of humankind. The Bible calls this Christian stubborn, stiff-necked, hard-hearted, and disobedient. Not Father's favorite person but, without argument, the one for whom Jesus died.

Willfully holding on and refusing to abandon spiritual and emotional pain arising from false, twisted belief systems based on lies originating from our own past traumatic human experiences has been, outside Adam's original sin, the most destructive transgression in shaping humankind's entire history of misery. (Read that sentence repeatedly, would you?)

The likes of Jezebel, Judas, Nero, Attila the Hun, Hitler, Stalin, Pol Pot, Jim Jones, 9/11, Columbine, Fort Hood, and the multitude of other school and church shootings, let alone the repeated downtown Chicago massacres are a scant few of the needy, wounded, unhealed, unrighteous, and deviant souls that quickly come to mind. Aren't these sad souls the shining examples of frank disobedience and dogged unwillingness to renew our minds (Romans 12:2, again) to line up with God's truth as the road to knowing His good, perfect, and acceptable will for godly and righteous living? Aren't we so often guilty of ignoring the cross and Jesus' offer for eternal life (John 17:3) while seeking our own ways to avoid all the inner healing ministers waiting patiently in the wings with Holy Spirit to help find the truth to set us free?

No wonder the Lord jumps at the chance to fix a slide projector, lawn mower, disabled vehicle, or CD player with a Kiss from Heaven. It's hard for a projector, mower, or CD player to go its own way. Gotta keep a closer eye, however, on a Toyota.

QUESTION: Where is the Kiss from Heaven in this God Story?

ANSWER: Are you surprised it has been years since God has fixed an inanimate object for Emily and me? Seems He is now trying to bring broken humanity into healing, wholeness, and holiness. That should be no surprise to anyone paying attention to the breakdown of our country's social structure, historically steeped in unified family, participatory community, preparatory education, constitutional governance, and abiding faith in God to one devolving into broken families, politically divided communities, propagandized schools, greedy governments, and an apostate church. How is that happening?

Why? Because our focus has sadly fallen from the "we" to the "me." We seem to willingly adhere less to constitutional principles based on God's Word and Christ's ethic of others-centeredness and individual self-sacrifice, which lead to unifying endpoints; instead, we have chosen to embrace secular-based principles of honoring diversity (identifying, recognizing, and exalting differences between us), which have led to division and a contrary but purposeful endpoint—authoritarian control rooted on the situation rather than constitutional control based on the document itself.* Is it a surprise after kicking God out of our public schools, higher education, local, state, and federal governments, media, social media, film industry, medicine, military, education, and, in limited instances, the churches themselves that the unchecked moral decay has risen to putrefying levels in society? If you were God, would you tarry for the abuse coming your way?

We are told, are we not, that Holy Spirit, the restrainer of lawlessness (2 Thess. 2:7), will withdraw Himself preceding the end times while apostasy and God-haters will arise with a vengeance. We can confidently assume that the reason lawlessness is steadily on the rise results from Holy Spirit restraining evil less and less. So, what does Jesus say about that? "But when these things begin to take place, straighten up and lift up your heads, because your redemption is drawing near" (Luke 21:28). So, isn't that our Kiss from Heaven in this God Story?

* The United States Supreme Court ruled on June 28, 2024, that "courts must exercise their independent judgment in deciding whether an agency has acted within its statutory authority" and "may not defer to an agency interpretation of the law simply because a statute is ambiguous." This solid ruling subjects agency decisions to the rigid checks and balances (that legislatures make laws and courts determine their constitutionality), leaving agency authority and perceived ambiguity less under the direct political biases of unelected bureaucrats and more to the indirect political biases of our legislatures and appointed judges which, thanks to the Constitution, are both subject to challenge as seen in the Chevron appellate decision mentioned above.

It Is Up To Him (1980/2012)

The Sa Kaeo Holding Center, a temporary refugee camp hastily constructed by October of 1979 near Thailand's border with Cambodia, was primarily meant—our Northwest Medical Team was told—to settle 42,000 Cambodian communist Khmer Rouge troops and families seeking asylum from Vietnamese forces in close pursuit. Swept along in the opportunistic wake of those Khmer insurrectionists were hordes of nationalist Cambodian civilians recently held hostage by those communists but now fleeing the latter's infamous "killing fields," vast areas of agricultural land illegitimately occupied by the Khmer Rouge to produce food by conscripted nationalist civilians forcefully driven from surrounding cities into cruel slave labor.

The Vietnamese had crossed into Cambodia's eastern frontier looking to not only eradicate those genocidal "killing fields" but to quell the politically violent anarchy perpetrated by the Khmer Rouge-controlled government in Phnom Penh, led by the maniacal Pol Pot, from further spilling its horrors into Vietnamese territory.

Nationalist refugees, weakened from months of slave labor, were sitting ducks for a wide range of tropical diseases (e.g., malaria, typhoid, and dengue fevers), various parasitic infestations, tuberculosis, gangrenous war wounds, and unrecognized in those early years, post-traumatic stress disorder (PTSD). Those conditions had plagued the refugees who had escaped the "killing fields" during their mountain passage to Thailand and were now ravaging the Rouge themselves.

Establishing Sa Kaeo

The Thai government had asked the UNHCR (United Nations High Commissioner for Refugees) to build Sa Kaeo overnight to house those unexpected hordes of Cambodians streaming across the border. Limited to a dry eleven-acre rice paddy with no source of fresh water, latrines were hastily dug in soil with inadequate drainage. So, while workers ceaselessly dug more pits and trenches, the mounting health hazard magnified in the already medically challenged community.

There were no effective ways to quarantine refugees ravaged by infectious diseases and infestations due to primitive conditions, poor sanitation, and lack of open space to separate the sick from the well. Exposure to severe climate changes, torrid sun to eventual monsoon rains, was unavoidable due to little or no protection from the elements. Blue plastic tarpaulins elevated by three- to four-foot-high wooden stakes eventually replaced newspapers and rags as the primary materials to create thousands of primitive but porous shelters, all rubbing shoulders with their crowded neighbors.

An Unforeseen Illness

Early one crystal morning in February 1980, there was an angry commotion among the Khmer Rouge following an unannounced purging of their Nationalist "hostages" from the camp under the guard of Thai troops seeking for them a more suitable, safer facility at the Khao I Dang camp a handful of miles away. A Rouge soldier had murdered a Cambodian civilian, not an altogether foreign event, during a controversy the previous evening, and emotions were running dangerously high on both sides. The air felt chilly that morning as we left our quarters, so I grabbed my veteran cold-weather Marine green flight jacket before walking a mile of pastureland dotted with peacefully grazing water buffalo (caribou) to the fenced limits of the camp while shivering the entire way. Surveying the Rouge, still raging over losing their "hostages," I noticed most were dressed in lightweight clothing.

Sweeping over me along with those mounting chills was the sudden reality: It was not the weather but the onset of fever that, despite my extensive list of immunizations and careful hygiene, was causing my symptoms. Not a surprise, was it, considering the paucity of Asian antibodies coursing through an average immunologically ill-prepared Westerner's bloodstream locked among this evolving public health disaster? Another team MD took my temperature; it registered 104 degrees Fahrenheit. That was not good. With no laboratory or X-ray facilities, the remaining doctors decided to "shotgun" the problem with IV quinine (the drug of choice against falciparum malaria at the time) along with broad-spectrum antibiotics to cover a wide range of bacterial infections. The team debated and then chose to treat their patient in the home where we lodged.

That home was owned and occupied by a local family who boiled caribou meat into dull gray silly putty for our team to eat six nights a week, roasted puppy dogs as a treat on the seventh, daily added mysterious vegetables and greens on the side (which I long suspected might be an excellent source of hepatitis A), and plied us with drinking water from sources unknown. The family also went way beyond the ordinary to offer us local color while we slept. A night's "sleep," really a vigil, amounted to stretching supine on thinly padded boards "accessorized" by a piece of camouflaged granite (no hyperbole here) masquerading as a pillow. Adding insults to injuries, directly beneath the floor of our crude but cozy "dormitory" lived a pair of 24-7 snuffling pigs and an insomniac rooster who never slept past three in the morning and was reliably punctual to announce it.

After lounging for a month between a rock and a hard place (sorry), wasn't the exhaustion from sleep deprivation coming from all that late-night oinking and early-morning cock-a-doodle-dooing alone a setup for illness? Then, while we are at it, let us toss in the incessant cackling of a score of nocturnal gecko lizards that frolicked all night among the rafters as heralds of a perfect tropical disease storm brewing on my horizon. So, at 10:00 a.m., with IVs hung, I dozed off into fitful sleep in the epicenter of Old MacDonald's farm. Suppertime arrived hand in hand with a fever of 105, incessant chills, and a cough with blood-tinged sputum. That spoke of hemorrhagic fever with pneumonia, not a good omen in the land of dengue fever or one of its various hemorrhagic cronies. So, after eloquently pleading my case, the team loaded me into a lorry destined for the Adventist hospital in Bangkok. An emergency department X-ray confirmed the pneumonia, the lab drew blood, and the hospital doctors admitted their patient to the medical floor. During the night, my temperature spiked to 106, an event coinciding with a descent into a coma.

On the Other End of the Thermometer

For the next few days, while shifting in and out of consciousness, I was intermittently alert enough to discover no one had put a medical finger on the cause. The doctors told my family in Oregon I carried a "guarded prognosis." Meanwhile, I remained puzzled at the surrounding gravity, feeling little but profound weakness from pneumonia when ascending to an occasional semi-conscious state. It was surreal to be in the twilight zone to hear voices discussing my condition but unable to respond. Over the next days, fear, helplessness, frustration, confusion, and waves of sorrow welled up, but I could not gain enough consciousness to voice my distress. Sensing a gentle pressure on my shoulder at those times, the anguish instantly lightened as I descended again into darkness.

Uncertain how often this sequence occurred each day, of this I am confident: Those contacts with a tangible touch brought an assurance someone was there standing with me, fighting alongside me, and not giving me up. Languishing in a deep place one day while hallucinating a beautiful multicolored but terrifying sea monster with a carnivorous grin, I was drowning in self-pity over my impotence as a prisoner of this condition.

Somewhere along the way, I handed my future to Jesus; within seconds, my failing medical condition and insecurity became unimportant as I resigned myself to Heaven if that was the Lord's wish. Then, at that precise moment, He spoke for the first and only time during my hospital stay: "You will never breathe another breath or take another step unless I ordain it."

That was it: short, sweet, to the point, profoundly simple, and a sober but comforting life-altering truth. I understood until entering glory, my life would be in the Lord's hands with Him deciding each breath and every step. No surprise, was it, that by the end of that day, I was sitting up in bed, the following in a wheelchair, and by the third, getting to my feet? A day later, weak, wobbly, and having lost twenty-six pounds, I left the hospital on a new mission. After discharge, the doctors reported my mother working her way toward Heaven from a hospital room in the States. Life had become a time of inexplicable irony.

Beyond the Medicine Cabinet

Arising like a phoenix from that coma, I met a petite angelic nursing student dressed in dark blue and assigned my bedside. Among her duties, I discovered, was to place her hand firmly but gently upon my shoulder anytime the coma "lightened" or I became agitated. She would never know what instantaneous comfort and unspeakable peace her touch gave during those desperate and uncertain times of struggle, although I tried earnestly for her to understand my profound gratitude.

Educated to the teeth and carrying a measure of diverse medical skills and a variety of experiences, I silently prided myself among the most important to be my bedside manner. Developing a reputation as a compassionate doctor drew scores of patients to our office stateside who appreciated kindness and concern in a physician-patient relationship. Though a caring heart is important, the one bottom-line measure of success in any physician's treatment was never so much caring as curing. Successful treatment demanded a cure. If a cure was not the endgame, then a doctor became no more than a compassionate cheerleader. Compassion was an essential tool and the means to an end in keeping patients engaged, encouraged, and comforted, but the end was to see the patient healed.

In this remote Bangkok Adventist facility, I was about to have an epiphany. Being imprisoned by that hospital bed and its coma revealed something contrary to my long-entrenched set of beliefs. When it was over, when the treatments failed, and the doctors had nothing more to offer, when I was overcome by fear, uncertainty, resignation, a broken will, and unmistakably certain there was no hope for a cure, I was finally primed for the most effective remedy known to man.

What was that but a gentle touch, a reminder in that medical prison of coma I was not alone; someone was reliably there, intently waiting for me to arise and ready to be a place of encouragement and comfort along the way. That touch became the light in my darkness, the cure-all for my shattered faith in medicine and its practitioners, allayed my fear and uncertainty, reconstituted my broken will, helped erase my feelings of resignation, and opened my door to hope.

Then, going beyond the comfort of the touch of another human came a deeper revelation: There is an even greater security in our times of trouble that goes beyond the hands of another human. It is only when compassionate Jesus touches us as our Healer, the One who ordains us to breathe, will we breathe, and to step will we move forward. So, without Him, we can do nothing (John 15:5b), but with Him, all things are possible (Matt. 19:26). If so, if we are always in His hands, is it not always up to Him? He and He alone decides the outcome but may use another's touch as His own to convey His ever-present care and a way to supply His comfort. Every good thing comes down from the Father of Lights, and it is His choice, not ours, where every good thing lands or does not land. It is simply up to us to praise Him for His willingness to not only choose on our behalf but for the choice He makes. Here, we learn a crucial lesson: We are in His wondrous hands, and He orchestrates each breath and step along the way until the end according to His will. Our place is merely to praise Him for His decisions because, in Him, all things work together for the ultimate good, i.e., completion, perfection, and maturity (Rom. 8:28).

A Reminder

Fast forward twenty-five years following that epiphany in Thailand and a time I set aside to be alone with the Lord. A friend suggested a Catholic Retreat, Lebh Shomea House of Prayer, near Sarita in South Texas. I was tucked into a small one-person cabin and under strict rules of silence, permissible to break only at morning mass (where the priest lost me), conducting work of absolute necessity in the business office, or counseling with the priest himself. So, I spent my days walking miles of wilderness, studying the Word, and praying. Though doing all the right things, alas, nothing was working.

Emily and I had become so busy ministering Ed Glaspey's wonderful Restoration Series (Christ Center, Junction City, Oregon) in three churches at once that the intimate presence of the Lord and the whole precious reason for the ministry had lifted from my life. What action I chose was to follow our Master's example and steal away to the Father (Mark 1:35). Brief as it was, I had stolen away but to no avail. So, after two days at the retreat and still feeling palpably distant from Jesus and His presence, I made an appointment with the priest. Our meeting was brief and to the point.

Father Kelly was a spiritual contemplative, I understood, but today first a listener. Hearing my whining over this recent lack of intimacy with Jesus needed little contemplation by my drive-by counselor.

He cut to the chase: "It is up to God," Father Kelly said confidently without emphasis or empathy, conservatively for the zillionth time in his life and with certainty the last time in mine.

That was it? No new epiphany? Guess not, for I had known that little message as an inescapable truth since that coma in Bangkok. Ah, but how soon we forget. Why are we fit to remember years and years of minutia from first grade, family secrets, social highlights and embarrassments, or Bible trivia but so quickly forget the life-changing revelation downloaded from warm-blooded experiences with our faithful Holy Spirit friend and mentor? Good question. Try this on for an answer: When Adam fell and the rest of us became cisterns that could hold no water (Jer. 2:13), it took Jesus's ascension for Holy Spirit to come and fill us with Himself (2 Cor. 13:5) and keep us in touch with Heaven. Like the lamps of those careless five virgins (Matt. 25:7–9), we can run dry of Him if we settle for less than ongoing fillings. Seeking encounters with Holy Spirit to remain "topped off" becomes not only our answer (Eph. 5:18), according to His perfect will (Jer. 29:13), but also guarantees that Holy Spirit will order our every step (Ps. 37:23) and ordain our every breath (Isa. 42:5).

PostScript

With that small avalanche of scriptures, no one here should need to travel around the globe to face a coma in a Thailand hospital or petition Heaven for a Mount Tabor-like tête-à-tête with dearly departed Father Kelly to be convinced that "It's up to Jesus." Believe me, to bypass a coma in that Bangkok hospital would qualify as a "Kiss from Heaven" all by itself. As for a Mount Tabor encounter with Father Kelly, that get-together would also be up to God, whether Moses and Elijah could find their way back with our Father Kelly the priest in tow, and we had enough left to conquer that way too big Mount Tabor ourselves. Know what? It might be far too long a trip for all of us, and let's be real: Nobody among this contingent is getting any younger.

Meanwhile, remember: "It's up to God," one ordained breath, one ordered step, and one Kiss from Heaven at a time. I hope I got it this time. How about you?

QUESTION: Where is the Kiss from Heaven in this God Story?

ANSWER: It was all up to God: illness, coma, an inner vision of a grinning enemy awaiting his turn, the bottom-line inner voice of Holy Spirit ensuring my steps and breaths would be forever ordered at His pleasure, as a compassionate comforter working through the hands of a gentle nursing student to allay my fears, and a release to come alongside my mother on her journey to Heaven. Mysteriously, had my struggle reduced her suffering? Would I have suffered for her? Of course. In an analogous mysterious way, did she give her life that I might keep mine? Would she have? Of course. What lovely thoughts. What beautiful possibilities. "Greater love has no one than this, that a person will lay down his life for his friends" (John 15:13).

A Hairy Situation (1982)

Mildred was as elderly as her name might suggest. In her mid-eighties, she was but one of my proud stable of aging geriatric lady patients who I loved beyond reason in Cottage Grove, Oregon. What treasures they were—rich with life's wisdom, God's grace, and overflowing with unrestrained affection and appreciation for my care, how could I not selfishly guard them as my own? Mildred, secretly, was my favorite. I never told one soul, but my staff not only knew this intuitively but demonstrably expressed their own similar prejudice whenever the old gal visited the office. It was with no small concern for all of us when Mildred developed malignant hypertension, defined as blood pressure exceeding 180/120 (mmHg).

Her medical condition soon became a medical conundrum. She had no symptoms, and urgent delivery of medication rapidly brought her to a safe range. All bloodwork and tests then proved within normal limits. Unfortunately, keeping her blood pressure in that safe range, even with a growing variety of antihypertensives, proved difficult. Having run through the drugs I was confident in using, I consulted a specialist in the not-so-big city of nearby Eugene. There was a medication he recommended, occasionally used in dire circumstances, which required two added separate prescription drugs to control its side effects. However, managed carefully by both doctor and patient, those three pharmaceuticals, working in combination, proved successful in controlling her hypertension.

Within a day or two, Mildred's blood pressure happily stabilized. What a relief to mitigate the potential for hemorrhagic stroke, myocardial infarction, congestive heart failure, and other threats she faced without adequate control. After daily checks and then weekly for a month, we scheduled her next appointment thirty days out with instructions to call if she noticed any further increase in her at-home blood pressure checks, adverse symptoms, or documented side effects from the medications.

A month later, as I was completing a visit with another patient, there arose a significant commotion in the waiting room. Reverberating throughout the entire clinic, boomed a voice. It belonged to Mildred: "Where is he; where is he? He has made me a monkey!" Oh, didn't I hurry to investigate. Rapidly shuffled out of earshot by my nurse to the nearest vacant exam room, the old girl was nowhere in sight. With increasing curiosity and mounting trepidation, I found her chart in the rack nearest her exam room door. Holding my breath, I entered the room only to stop short, look twice at Mildred, and, finally, an unbelieving third time. Oh my, the old gal was spot-on; I had made her a monkey. Honestly, on closer inspection, she looked more like a scaled-down version of a silverback gorilla.

Oh, the beautiful, brilliant silver-gray shocks of hair piled high over her head, growing down her neck, across a nearly hidden forehead, temples, and buried ears only to surge like an avalanche over once unoccupied cheeks as lush sideburns cascading south into a magnificent goatee, now camouflaging a hidden chin resting somewhere in its depths below. Arising to face me, the long silver hairs from her outstretched forearms drifted ever so gently in stark contrast to her gnarled index fingers waggling in my direction as if a disgruntled second-grade teacher confronting an intractable student. It was a surreal moment, sifted, it seemed, from among the less-memorable scenes of *Mighty Joe Young, Planet of the Apes*, and a variety of other vintage B-rated monkey movies.

Well, don't you know I had to talk fast. Reminding Mildred of our earlier discussions on how excess hair growth was a required reportable side effect of her medication (among others, which we covered thoroughly again on the spot), I incoherently rambled on that she had been instructed to call with any side effects while again emphasizing she must learn to follow her doctor's instructions. Meanwhile, Mildred, during my entire tirade to remind her of my past reminders, was incessantly reminding me I had made her a monkey, and all she wished was to be a human again.

Reluctantly, with Mildred's perfect blood pressure tinged with my disappointment, I wisely tapered her medication over the next few weeks while referring her to that bigger city hypertension specialist to clean up this mess. Six weeks of new medication later, Mildred, now recognizable and loosed from all that excess body foliage, had again achieved a respectable blood pressure—although, I submit, not so respectable as when I had made her a monkey.

Postscript

Did you miss investing in Amazon, Google, Microsoft, Netflix, and Apple? I did. Well, I had Netflix for a while but sold it for Studebaker or something as inane. Oh, there was one similar, although slightly smaller, missed opportunity I need to also confess. In 1982, Loniten was the trade name of Mildred's antihypertensive medication. From the late eighties into the early nineties, doctors began prescribing Rogaine to their patients as a topical medication for hair growth. You nailed it, friend; the generic name for both Loniten and Rogaine is minoxidil, earlier that monkey-making high blood pressure pill and later a money-making topical medication for hair growth.

Way before Upjohn laboratories saw Rogaine emerge from its longtime patented pharmaceutical Loniten (minoxidil), our Mildred (and 85 to 90 percent of all Loniten users by later report) had suffered one significant side effect, hypertrichosis (excessive hair growth), prompting the pharmaceutical industry to pounce upon this unforeseen opportunity to create a safe topical hair restoration product and veritable cash cow. Years later, the public could buy Rogaine (minoxidil) in topical form by prescription and, finally, as an over-the-counter medication.

Well, along with countless others, I missed Mildred's inadvertent broadcasting of her medication's potential as both a "killer" hair restoration product and a rare investment opportunity. Nor did I recognize this potential when a large living room mirror, standing upright across the entire rear seat of my big brown wrinkled Suburban, reflected a bald spot half the size of Rhode Island on the back of my own bright and shiny dome smack dab onto Big Brown's rearview mirror on an equally bright and shiny Saturday morning. Taking immediate action, I switched from combing my hair from side to side to front to back in a valiant but futile effort to camouflage that barren waste site for the next forty years, put a little more money into "Studebaker," and wouldn't you know, missed another potential investment opportunity, Rogaine.

There was one Kiss from Heaven for which a bunch of alert market investors and a vast number of chrome domes, excluding yours truly, owe a bunch of kudos to a whole community of unaware, unintended, and unrewarded longhaired beta-tested guinea pigs like our sweet Mildred for their company's good fortune. After all my flubs surrounding this hairy situation, aren't you curious as to where my Kiss from Heaven comes from in this story? Only because you never knew my Mildred. Let's look a little deeper.

QUESTION: Where is the Kiss from Heaven in this God Story?

ANSWER: In Romans 16:13, the Apostle Paul writes, "Greet Rufus, a choice man in the Lord, also his mother and mine." Now, Rufus was allegedly the son of Simon the Cyrene, a Black man from North Africa who carried Jesus's cross to Golgotha but later lived in Antioch. When Barnabas fetched Paul to that city from his isolation in Tarsus (having earlier been sent via Caesarea to that Cilician town by the Christian community after stirring up Jerusalem with his unflappable witness), it seems Rufus's mother may have been an important part of Paul's healing, restoration, and readiness for his first missionary journey. In similar ways was my Mildred, without her knowing, a mother to me during my fledgling days of medical practice in Oregon (a lovely missionary journey by itself) and another enduring and blessed Kiss from Heaven in this God Story.

A Little Poupouri Of Father's Love (1984)

Chinese food and I, like so many close relationships between two well-meaning folks at any age, fell into an unintended funk in my early fifties when an unresolvable conflict arose between my blood pressure and its MSG (monosodium glutamate). There is no uncomplicated way to describe the painful fallout from this sad state except to say it had become a love affair, once sweet, gone sour (sorry). Then, predictably, like couples who care for each other but just cannot live together, egg rolls, Mar Far chicken, fried rice, and I would occasionally falter into unreal expectations and steal away for a brief evening's delight. Predictably, these trysts would quickly lead to satisfying, although brief, afterglows, which just as rapidly deteriorated into whopping hypertensive headaches. On this path one evening, I was about to join a group of friends for an early dinner at the Ocean Sky, a Chinese eatery in the south part of town. Fooling myself again and still living in "La-La Land," I was fantasizing once more as if the past were behind us and it would all work out.

Before we go further, I have two questions to pose: The first is, "For what reason do we insanely keep doing the things we keep doing when we keep getting the things we keep getting?" Good question without enough time for a satisfactory answer or getting it to stick. So, let us move to the second: "Why did Holy Spirit show up in that parking lot like an unscheduled patient ambushing me with a 'By the way, doctor, while I have you here,' when I was simply looking for supper and a little social downtime?" It was hardly a spiritual moment unless considering that the upcoming heavenly Mar Far chicken might qualify. It would not have been a moment I would have picked. Still, true to form and out of the blue (actually, the late Oregon winter's drizzly gray) burst this polished gem from the heart of Jesus. Now, this is a graphic picture, so unless you have a strong stomach or have finished your Mar Far chicken, do dessert first.

"If today," Holy Spirit began, and I paraphrase, "they came for you and took you to a fortified place from which you would never return—not to loved ones, friends, your church, your profession, or your business—and led you to its deepest subterranean recesses where no light or sound penetrated and there, stripped naked, they took your sight and hearing, removed your tongue, broke your hands, feet, extremities, and back, and then tortured your mind endlessly so that, finally, alone and lying in the cold, dark deafening silence where you would never again read my Word, hear my Spirit, utter My name, comfort another with your touch, share My good news, bear anyone's burden, or ever consider, remember, or understand a thing about your Lord and Savior for the remainder of your life, would I, your Father God, love you any less? Would I love you any less than I do my Son, Jesus? The answer, my child, is no! Altogether, no!"

How this simple (well, maybe not-so-simple) epiphany from Holy Spirit changed my understanding of Father God's love for me. In the space of heartbeats, it set me free from legalism, conditions, traditions, rules, and regulations, "musts," "shoulds," "oughts," and all the perfectionistic striving, driving, and conniving that for so long had kept me feeling conditionally condemned and too often at arm's length from my Lord. Suddenly, I knew that not one thing under Heaven could ever separate me from the love (Rom. 8:31–39) and presence of my God (Ex. 33:14), that His love for me was unencumbered, without qualification, and freely given. God loved me, it seemed, without a single condition, any hesitation, and for no good reason.

Doesn't that do something down deep in you? Can't you just feel the chains popping, the fetters dropping, the condemnation stopping, and the prison doors swinging wide? No more bondage to effort, performance, looking good, getting it right, or being numero uno! Why? Because in the Lord's eyes, you are already top of the class, the teacher's pet, the apple of His eye, His special treasure, and a favored child of the King. There is nowhere else to go from here but down, and that will not happen because He has bought you with a price, called you by name, lifted you from the miry clay, branded you with His Spirit, written your name on the palm of His hand, and has promised to never leave, forsake, or allow you out of His sight. Now, friend, doesn't that sound like somebody seriously in love with you?

Entitlements and Privileges

Here are irrefutable statements: God's love is an entitlement, and everybody can receive it without condition. Did you know that? God's love is available as a gift! We can spurn it, but we cannot earn it. Consider this: We need not even believe that He exists to be eligible for His love. That is true; study John 3:16, "For God so loved the world . . ." That passage doesn't say, "For God so loved the believers or even the religious," does it? Guess what? God's love extends to the correct, the incorrect, the politically correct, and even to His enemies. God's love is "inclusive." Must we belong to His Church to receive His love? No. Nor must we profess Christ as our Lord and Savior. Am I serious? Dead serious!

Oh, not that the Father's heart does not long for all of humanity to receive Jesus as Lord and depend on Him as Savior. Look, Father wants to wipe all our slates clean; He is the God of the second chance. He wants to forgive our faults, failures, mistakes, faux pas, and sins to reconcile every difference that has kept us from Him. Why? So we can come to spend an intimate eternity with Him. That means

Heaven, my friend, and not just Heaven above but Heaven on Earth, where He welcomes us into His presence. When we embrace and follow Christ, that is the outcome. Miraculously, that is all it takes. What is the downside? Well, it is both simple and scary. When we do not make that choice, Heaven will not happen. Are we to understand that if we choose another path God will love us less? No. Will He turn His back on us? Absolutely not! Will His heart break over our choice of destiny? Be certain. Our choice to remain separate denies Him the opportunity for reconciliation and restoration of a two-way intimate love relationship with us.

Reconciliation and restoration, if you have not already noticed, are the ultimate desires of Father's heart. Distressing to consider, is it not, that our reluctance to partake in His reconciliation is keeping humankind estranged from Him. Does that mean He is closer to His children than those who refuse to come to Him in Christ, the One who has made this reconciliation possible? Most certainly. But because we are closer to our own children who spend more time with us than those who are distant or even estranged does not mean we love our "prodigals" any less, does it? By no means. It shows there is a painful gulf between us, a separation that inhibits the expression of mutual love. How often do we see Christians agonizing over the life choices of their "prodigals," spending time in prayer for their return, and wishing to restore relationships with them? The Father's great commission has the identical intent. Reconciliation and restoration of His relationships with His missing and estranged children is foremost in His heart, crucially important to His joy, and the entire reason He gave up His only Son to that cruel cross on Calvary.

Smitten over Some Flea-Bitten Rover

So, becoming a Christian never gives us a corner on God's love, only on His intimacy. God's love, as we have seen, is unconditional. His intimacy is not. Here is a quick analogy in no way intending to trivialize the love of the Father: I am a dog lover, an unabashedly passionate, out-of-the-closet dog lover with the T-shirts to prove it. Always have been and always will be! Could not imagine it any other way. I commonly cross streets to socially introduce myself to dogs: fancy dogs, hybrids, or mutts; it makes no difference. Dogs in cars or on leashes, junkyard dogs, friendly dogs, or mean dogs; it does not matter. As a kid, I would sneak every homeless pooch I could scrounge up into the house and, believe me, I scrounged up a bunch. Often flea-infested with the pungent perfume of an overcrowded kennel, my bedroom drove my poor mother half-crazy, but I could not help myself. I was driven. I was intense. I was focused. Always smitten over some flea-bitten rover. That was my lot.

My own folks did not get it. Nor did our family dog, who, above all, should have had a little empathy. After expressing hostility to each new canine interloper, the family pooch would suffer from self-pity or depression. "Get a life, dog," I would preach, "you have it made. Make room at the inn, Fido! Out there are dogs to love, dogs to save, and dogs to bring home." To my dismay and my dog's glee, a number of my boarders left on their own. Sadly, in search of them, I found few. Do you get my drift? I not only loved dogs but had to have them close. Still, as painful as it was for me, I understood that it was up to them to stay or hit the road. Our Father understands such things, too. But that does not mean he stops looking, loving, hoping, and grieving.

Because of Him or Because of Us?

The Lord is like that with humans. He is crazy about us and wants to take us all home, immerse us in His Name, cleanse us with His blood, adopt us into His family, and draw us into ongoing fellowship with Him forever. Look, God really cannot help Himself. Nor would He try. He is immutable, unchangeable. He will not and cannot deny who He is. And who does the Bible say He is? God is love (1 John 4:16). It is who He is and what He does. He created us to be His outlets for and objects of His love. We fulfill Him when He fulfills us. Look, what good is love without a way for its expression? No matter who we are, what we do, where we live, what we believe, or how clean, dirty, rich, poor, kind, or nasty we are, one truth stays: God loves us not because of who we are but because of who He is—unrestrainable love. Let me rephrase this: God's love for us is not about us being lovable, valuable, special, merited, or worthy of love; instead, it is about God fulfilling His own identity, need, purpose, and destiny. We must see this clearly: It is all about Him, His will, and His ways; again, it is about who He is and not about who we are.

That God would sacrifice His son to reconcile and restore a relationship with sinners who ignored, mocked, or hated Him is incomprehensible. It must convince us He is the most humble, wonderful, kind, considerate, unselfish, forgiving, and loving person we could ever meet. Who would be crazy enough not to covet His friendship, His love, His intimacy, His eternal companionship, and to become His child? Who would be so deranged to bypass Heaven? Yet, if, in our stubborn mental illness, pride, rebellion, and stiff-necked sin, we go our own way and never give Him another thought, He still honors our choice to leave; still, He will steadfastly grieve and continue to pursue us, to court us, and try to draw us back into an intimate loving relationship. Why? Because He is who He is and cannot deny Himself. He is love, and love's purpose and destiny are to seek expression, satisfaction, and fulfillment in a relationship with a lover: I am my beloved's, and He is mine (Song of Sol. 6:3). More than anything, He wishes us with Him, sharing His presence, and allowing Him to love us intimately. Forgive me for the preceding rambling stream of Christian consciousness. What follows is but a brief living sliver of what I am trying to impart.

A Night to Remember

In the mid-1980s, I returned from another few weeks of ministry in Mindanao, the second largest of the Philippine islands, where our team had watched God do countless miracles and bring scores of beautiful Filipinos to Himself. Exhausted and having yet to overcome a severe case of jet lag, I was wandering our expansive Oregon country property beneath a glorious star-studded sky at 2:30 a.m. on a moonless spring morning. Needing a good night's sleep, my clock was still topsy-turvy and would not cooperate. Hoping the fresh air had helped, I entered an empty bedroom, vacated when my eldest daughter left for college, and promptly fell into a deep sleep.

Waking within minutes, I intuitively knew there was something or someone in the room. Gradually, I became aware of a sweet, unidentifiable fragrance seeping into the pitch-black silence of my world beneath the bedcovers. Bathed in its captivating presence, I lay motionless for minutes, fearing its loss.

First cautious, then curious, I was driven to experience the origin of this captivating essence. Incrementally inching the bedclothes toward my neck, in a nanosecond, that unidentifiable bouquet, now a weighty tsunami of pure love, unceremoniously pinned me as would a wrestler to my mattress. Under its weightiness, I could not move, nor did I wish to. With the heaviness, anxiety rose in my chest; then, simultaneously, came a competing state of perfect peace and safety. There, locked in that emotional paradox, my little world paused as if in suspended animation.

Over an indeterminate time, my mind caught its breath; I recall thinking this must be His rest, the place of perfect peace in God that defies human understanding. Repeatedly inhaling intentional breaths carried the intoxicating fragrance deeply into my body and spirit, further saturating me with peace. Oddly enough, I never entertained the obvious: The Lord was in my room, and I was in His Glory. Nor did I question why He was there or consider waking anyone else in the home to talk about it. Reclining there, soaking in His presence, feeling a little inebriated, and a prisoner of His unconditional love, intimacy, peace, and the person of Jesus was more than enough.

How long I was submersed in His glory and saturated with the fragrance of Him, I do not know. What I knew was nothing, absolutely nothing else mattered. Absolutely nothing. Barely able to think or reason, my only quest was to remain motionless in the wonder of that unsurpassable moment.

Melting in His fragrance, wanting to be with Him alone, and to be completely and only His was everything. I also sensed He felt the same. With jetlag gone, at daybreak I awoke more refreshed than ever before in my life. Somewhere during that overwhelming interlude, I had slipped off into the comfort of the deep, peaceful sleep He gives His beloved (Ps.127:2). Not to this day have I known His intimacy again in this manner or to that degree. A potpourri of unforgettable moments to bless His child would have to last for decades. And, as you can see, it has.

Postscript

Immersion in God's glory is a life-changing experience in this way: You are never again satisfied with the ordinary. Those few moments under His presence were the coalescence of His welcome, perfect peace, safety, rest, unconditional love, acceptance, connection, intimacy, and oneness in our relationship. It was experiencing "eternal life," knowing the Father and Jesus in the fullest measure (John 17:3). Hadn't He done this before by hovering first over creation and then His servant Mary to bring life in other ways? It has always been about Him extending Himself in creative moments when our willingness to be still and receive His loving presence brings forth new life.

Have you ever questioned if the elders in Heaven prostrate before God's throne are less in that position due to His power and their powerlessness than revealing Father's desire for an extended time of quiet intimacy with His children? Then, are we to view Jesus on the cross as a determined effort by an obedient Son to please His Father or the greatest attempt at reconciliation, expression of love, and quest for ultimate intimacy ever visited by Heaven upon all humankind? Was the transformation of a fearful, crushed, and cowardly Peter into a mighty man of God by the *dunamis* of the Spirit at Pentecost to manifest the Father's surpassing power to save and deliver or His way to restore love, intimacy, and oneness to a single broken fisherman? When Jesus struck down, blinded, and had murderous Saul carried as an invalid into Damascus to meet Ananias, was that the result of the righteous right arm of Jehovah delivering a public rebuke for Saul's sins of abuse and homicide or more that wicked man's first step into a baptism of Father's love, reconciliation, restoration, intimacy, and destiny?

All the manifest encounters with the Spirit of God I have experienced or that have been shared with me by others, when I look at them from Abba's perspective, have been underlying expressions of His love to help draw us closer to Him. Can we see how Father's Great Commandment to love manifests His supreme desire to reconcile and unify with humankind by way of His Great Commission, spreading the gospel of His lovingkindness by inexplicable, extraordinary, and supernatural miracles throughout the earth to seek intimate union and oneness with every soul lost in this dark world?

This epiphany may be easier to accept if God's presence has pinned you to your mattress for a short season on a long, lovely Oregon spring night to receive a genuinely fragrant Kiss from Heaven. Oh, how I pray that might be your experience too.

QUESTION: Where is the Kiss from Heaven in this God Story?

ANSWER: There is mention of the fragrance of Christ (2 Cor. 2:15) emanating from Christians who reach out to others and God to sacrifice in love (Eph. 5:2). Does this mean that Holy Spirit is showing us how He clothes us in the aroma of Christ when we lay our lives down for others (i.e., here, my journey to the Philippines)? Countless testimonies of saints having experienced that fragrance when drawing near Him during intense times of worship or while loving others sacrificially have been documented. I have no proof that my profound time in that bedroom's fragrance was for either reason or even a heavenly visitation . . . unless you agree being simultaneously pinned to a mattress by Abba's weightiness (*kavod*) for a season of oneness may have been supporting evidence enough. Always has been for me and, of course, the Kiss from Heaven in this story.

A Pair of Susans (1992)

Susan was a gravely ill school psychologist in her mid-thirties. A lovely Christian woman with an ugly metastatic disease, her cancer had long ago left its secret hiding places and was now ostentatiously parading victory, even while Susan was holding on to her healing by faith. Progressively paler, emaciated, and indisputably weakened with no family nearby, she was spending her days sharing a small but comfortable home with a good friend and benefactor, another Susan. The home had become the center of our nightly prayer sessions, a resource for hurting Christians who needed a touch from their Master. Psychologist Susan's arrival extended the ministry and presented the Lord with another opportunity to perform an attesting miracle. Over the ensuing weeks, His wonderful presence filled our meetings as our new arrival opened herself to Holy Spirit and, soon enough, found strength to minister to the rest. Packed into a tiny living room, exalting the Lord with simple praise choruses, and bathing those willing in sweet prayer, we watched Holy Spirit ready Susan's heart for the Lord's perfect will.

The Advent of Benny Hinn

Before long, we discovered that Benny Hinn, each of our Susan's favorite televangelist, was bringing his crusade to Casey Treat's megachurch in Tacoma, Washington. But five hours away from Eugene, Oregon, Benny's visit offered a splendid opportunity to fulfill one of both our Susan's fondest dreams. The meeting would bless them while offering the Lord another chance to heal our desperately ill sister. Friends and owners of a large recreational vehicle agreed to supply transportation, so we scheduled departure for high noon on the day of Benny's meeting.

That morning, Susan's condition had deteriorated, being weaker but also in demonstrably more pain. While I had taken the day from work to manage her care, our pastor had reserved a space in Casey Treat's sanctuary where Susan would have a clear view of Benny's platform from her wheelchair. We were ready, but was our patient? Gathering around her bed and trying to carry her to the RV proved a formidable task. Repeated attempts to lift Susan from her bed provoked increasingly severe distress. Sadly, after doses of analgesics and two hours devoted to devising pain-free ways to lift her, we yielded to the anguish and, reluctantly, admitted defeat. One thing became clear: Though illness canceled our dear Susan's Tacoma adventure, she needed time to prepare for her upcoming one to Heaven. It is hard to describe the painful ambivalence of our little flock's feelings in so many ways surrounding so many things that morning.

When Susan sunk into an exhausted sleep, we retired to the living room while struggling to reconcile ourselves to this setback. For days, our crew had eagerly awaited this upcoming venture with the anticipation of a child awaiting Christmas. Fatigued from working days and ministering nights, the trip had further offered all a needed respite. But the bulk of our disappointment centered on Susan's profound heartbreak over missing Benny and a visit that might have offered her a healing touch from Jesus. Any who knew Benny Hinn, whatever their questions, doubts, private opinions, or Christian persuasion, had to admit that healing miracles were common to his ministry. Missing this meeting, we understood, meant missing one more chance for Susan's survival. Time moved on as we sat in the little living room, re-hashing the whys and wherefores of our communal shattered dream.

A Ride of Faith

It was past 2:00 p.m. when our host Susan had a grand idea: Why not take patient Susan's favorite long-waisted T-shirt to Tacoma for the laying on of Benny's hands? Who could forget Apostle Paul's hand-kerchiefs sent from the school at Tyrannus (Acts 19:12) meeting with immeasurable healings? How my spirit leapt; count me in! Checking the clock, it was 2:20 p.m., and we were five hours from a meeting that started in four hours and forty minutes. Snatching patient Susan's shirt and racing for host Susan's little blue Honda car, we sped away. Could we make it? The bigger question was could we make it in time?

Approaching the weekend, Interstate 5, running north from Eugene, turned out to be a logjam as we forged over the McKenzie River toward Portland. Keeping to the speed limit would snatch defeat from the jaws of victory. Having little choice to find room at the meeting if we arrived after 7:00 p.m., we pegged the speedometer at an unchristian eighty miles per hour. Approaching the Woodburn exit south of Portland, with a sinking heart, I recognized the familiar wide-brimmed hat of an Oregon State Trooper at the exact time we swept past his unmarked police car. "Oh, Lord, we are done, finished, and cooked. It's over," I moaned with my companion adding an amen. Foot free from the accelerator and slowing without using the brakes (as if the trooper had not seen my contrails) with resign, I checked the rearview mirror for his oncoming flashing lights. What I saw was the patrol car sliding off the freeway at the last exit. "Wow, thank you, Jesus. What a wonder!" Celebration filled the car.

Snail pacing through the late afternoon Portland rush-hour traffic created an unforeseen delay, which stole any minutes we had gained during our mad dash from Eugene. With the die cast and the Rubicon crossed (well, at least the Columbia), there was no turning back. I thought about that unobservant trooper. Could it be that the Lord had blinded his eyes? Other such episodes crossed my mind; Peter being led past the prison guards by the angel headed the list (Acts 12:9–10). Having rocketed by that officer at this high rate of speed had seemed like a defiant "in-your-face" act, didn't it? Was the Lord giving us favor, even while we intentionally broke the law? I futilely sought other biblical examples. That answer would have to wait—but not for long.

Not far into Washington, we were powering around a curve straightening out beneath a freeway overpass. There, secluded in the shelter of its concrete columns, sat side-by-side Washington State patrol cars occupied by troopers engaged in conversation. We flashed by them with no chance at all to decelerate. "Okay," I moaned again, "we have tested God, and here comes the reckoning." The cruisers did not move. Were the troopers finishing their chat before the chase? It appeared not. Something extraordinary was happening: The Lord wanted us in Tacoma. "We will make it in time," I confidently asserted, "no doubt about it." Susan added her "amen."

Another Hurdle

Reaching the outskirts of Tacoma found our overheated little Blue Honda taking the first possible exit as much to put this impromptu NASCAR event through a checkered flag as to find that Benny Hinn meeting. While decelerating off the exit ramp, we discovered that neither of us knew the location or name of Casey's church. Susan suggested, "Let's stop at a gas station for directions."

A little bit exasperated with this feminine logic that expected a convenience store teeny bopper in nowheresville to be privy to the location of a Benny Hinn meeting (In 1992, Benny was yet to become a household name), I impatiently awaited my friend's return from that wild goose chase as a chance to continue our own. Within moments, Susan arrived with detailed written directions to the church; I said nothing because I had nothing to say. The episodes with patrol cars had taught me a little, but not enough; no question now that the Lord was at the helm of this mission. It was precisely 7:00 p.m. when we stumbled past a church parking lot overflowing onto a street lined with cars as far as the eye could see. At the entrance to the over-crowded sanctuary, a security guard tersely waved us north to an overflow building equipped with a video screen. Unready to accept that fate, we informed the gatekeeper of our pastor's past reservations, explaining why patient Susan was absent and how we hoped to have Benny anoint her T-shirt for healing. He enthusiastically called the lead usher, and within seconds, we were weaving our way, shirt in hand, through the crowded sanctuary only to end up pressed against its hinder parts and a country mile from the platform. By far not the best seat in the house, was it? But by now, we were confident. The Lord was making a way where there was no way.

Here Comes Benny

Within minutes, Benny arrived. His first line of business was to invite those against the back wall of the sanctuary to come forward to an area inexplicably devoid of humanity and directly in front of the platform. That meant us. So, within seconds, we were ten feet from the action. Ten feet!

What a glorious night filled with worship and ministry focused on needy Christian Russian immigrants followed. Benny, pausing at one point in his familiar fashion, asked if the crowd wanted a touch from the Lord. A resounding "yes!" was the echo. With a broad sweep of Benny's arm, a sizable section of the audience before him fell under the Spirit's power. Whoa! Double whoa!

All this activity was at the far-right side of the platform. Strategically snaking through the crowd along its leading edge while carrying Susan's shirt took me into Benny's line of sight. Now, I schemed, even if the evangelist neglected to lay hands upon the shirt, I had positioned myself where, were he to "sweep the presence" over the audience again, the shirt might get a "dose." Even at that moment, the scheme felt a little far-fetched, but I reasoned that desperate times demanded desperate measures. Realistically, I was holding on by mustard seed faith but believing God still had a plan.

Happily, within minutes, Benny was standing but ten feet away where, for the second time that evening, he was asking if God's people wished a touch from the Lord. A booming multitude of amens readied him for action; Benny wound up and prepared to deliver the anointing.

Cookies and Kisses

My walk as a born-again Christian began as a worn-out thirty-four-year-old in a small traditional Christian church in Southern California during the waning years of the Jesus Movement. For an adult at that age, salvation is statistically a miracle. Hardened I was, in serial ways, a Vietnam veteran trying unsuccessfully to discover anesthesia for the disillusionment in my life. Like countless others seeking peace, I had sought other paths, so why not Jesus? Over the following years, the Lord mysteriously included in my walk a litany of inexplicable, if not supernatural, experiences. I often wondered if those events were not to guard against my penchant for worldliness or, more likely, to reign in my independent ways.

Often, those experiences followed obedience to the Lord's wishes or behaving in a way known to please Him. At other times, they felt like a sudden cookie given me by my mother only because she loved me. In no way am I trivializing Father's ways, but illustrating that our Abba is intensely personal, creative, and knows not only what keeps us connected to Him but also the most effective ways to deliver them. Having christened those interactions with Father as Kisses from Heaven, there could be no better way to illustrate His wonderous ways than by what was about to happen in Tacoma.

Kitty Hawk in Tacoma

Benny Hinn stood poised for action. On "shirt alert," I had lifted patient Susan's garment heavenward with my right arm at the same moment Benny's arm swept forward. "Take that," he boomed, omitting his standard (and somewhat less than believable) "whooshing" imitation of a mighty rushing wind. When nothing happened after a millisecond, my mind said, "Well, whatever!" Truly, that was my exact "faith-filled" thought. Oh, doesn't that sound like a predictable response from a guy never knocked off his pins by Holy Spirit?

Despite my willingness to seek the Lord on behalf of Susan, I remained a tad cynical. Why? Well, I had been around Charismatics and Pentecostals for fifteen years and had watched my share of bodies hit the deck. Legitimate or illegitimate, I had no opinion for any other reason than it was never my experience. Thomas the Doubter, I recall, was hewn from that same log. And since it had never been my lot, I was not ready to make a judgment. If the Lord wished to make me a believer in this arena, it would be up to Him. The ball was in His court.

In a flash, it was in mine as I was elevated off the carpet, the toes of my shoes bouncing off it all the way to the first row of chairs fifteen feet from lift-off. Deposited abruptly in one of them, I was, as you too might have been, justifiably confused. What had happened? Well, I had defied gravity. Not possible. Yet here I was, sitting squarely in the first row after a "flight," I will admit, a tad shorter bond less world-changing than Kitty Hawk's. In my world, however, it was, "Move over, Orville!"

Wait a second; something beneath my "tuther-end" did not feel normal. Glancing over my left shoulder, I saw a most astonished woman's face. It was for a good reason: I was sitting in her lap. Leaping aloft while profusely spewing apologies to both her and her husband, Benny's voice boomed over the sound system again, "You, the fellow with the shirt, come up and bring your wife." Now, I was even more confused; I had a shirt but no wife. Benny picked this up; "Come up and bring that couple with you." The three of us climbed the platform, the woman and her husband going directly to Benny while someone shuffled me elsewhere. Peculiarly, I was feeling unusually happy. Maybe a little buzzed.

Shortly, Benny beckoned, and we moved toward each other. Three feet apart, he "whooshed" the microphone and, like an unstrung marionette, I crumpled to the floor in a tangled heap. Was that me giggling? What was that about? A worker looking down said, "Got a bit of a dose, did we?" A bit? No, it was not; I was wasted. Trying to crawl on my hands and knees toward the front of the platform (for who knows what reason besides my lack of sobriety), I heard Benny question, "Where is the guy with the shirt?" Good Samaritans helped usher me to the microphone, where Benny asked about our mission. I babbled Susan's story while, hands upon the shirt, Benny prayed. I do not recall it as a prayer for healing but for blessing and peace. Then, at point-blank range, he blew directly on me again. Down I went like a sack of potatoes, giggling like a little girl in a tickle fit.

Do you remember Peter, after Holy Spirit showed up at Pentecost, saying that the people were not drunk with wine as his detractors supposed since it was but nine o'clock in the morning (Acts 2:15)? Well, it may not have been as they supposed, but believe me, they were drunk. There I was rolling and slithering my way to the stairs leading from the platform where, sprawled along the second stair from the top, I lay willing but not successful to sober up.

Okay, the Lord had made me a believer. I had been "slain in the Spirit" for the first time. It had happened, so I now could form an opinion; whatever that experience, I opined in my inebriated state, it more than exceeded my criteria for a glorious Kiss from Heaven.

From Benny Then to Jesus

In less than an hour, the meeting adjourned and, approaching my right mind, Susan and I began our long journey back to Eugene. Interrupted but once for a power nap, we were approaching 6:00 a.m. when the little blue Honda car reached home. Shirt in hand, my friend Susan disappeared through her front door. There, before helping patient Susan into her newly anointed burial garment, she shared the story about our night's glorious Benny Hinn crusade with her enthralled but failing friend hanging on every word. Moments later, perfectly at rest, our dear sister peacefully slipped away into the waiting arms of her Great Physician.

Postscript

My "Kitty Hawk" experience is the type of anecdote that drives the "Miracles are not for today" crowd crazy, running for their Hank Hanegraaff Bibles and assigning its origin to everything from mental illness to fulminating demonization (which is also not for today). Now, these folks intentionally detour around the Apostle Paul and his fire-breathing contingent found "fallen to the ground" (Acts 26:14) in an encounter with Holy Spirit on the road to Damascus, the mobs "drawing back and falling to the ground" (John 18:6) in Gethsemane when apprehending Jesus, the guards "becoming as dead men" (Matt. 28:4) at Christ's tomb in the presence of the angel, and the priests wobbling around and unable to stand under the cloud as Solomon dedicated the temple (1 Kings 8:10–11). Then scriptures like "Jesus Christ is the same yesterday, today and forever" (Heb. 13:8) and "Truly, truly, I say to you, he who believes in Me, the works that I do shall he do also; and greater works than these shall he do; because I go to the father" (John 14:12) raise more thorny issues surrounding being "slain in the Spirit" in today's Church.

Even if we ignore countless identical events recorded by history over the last two thousand years, how do we rationalize the elders pasted like postage stamps to the floor around the throne of God in the book of Revelation at this very moment? Here is one truth: When God shows up, men go down. Call it enforced reverence, prescribed rest, a time of intimacy, or whatever you like; it has, however, been a rule of thumb whenever the Spirit of the Living God has confronted men for ages.

Anyone who has had a supernatural encounter with Holy Spirit accompanied by manifestations would tell you this: Miracles will never save you, but they can build your faith in Jesus, gratitude for His personal ministry, and a testimony of His presence in our lives. Being "slain in the Spirit" (a descriptive phrase similar in metaphorical ilk to "trinity" and "rapture," neither of which can be found in the Bible) has occurred as humans have experienced God's presence for centuries. It is also but one of a series of manifestations which may occur. Biblically, think of Phillip's transport, Enoch's translation, Moses' shining face, Sampson's superhuman strength, Jacob's wrestling match, Solomon's wisdom, Elijah's chariot, all the prophets' verifiable prophecies, angelic visitations, Jesus' many miracles, resurrection, and ascension, Pentecost's mighty wind, fire, and conversions, Peter's angelic jailbreak and healing shadow, Lazarus's resurrection, Stephen's vision, Paul's healing handkerchiefs at Tyrannus and raising a young man from the dead, Ananias and Sapphira's peculiar deaths, and John's revelation on the Lord's day as but some of the evidence of what can happen when Heaven touches Earth.

People fall out for aberrant reasons. Sometimes it is wishful thinking and sometimes hyper-spirituality. Sometimes it is for attention, and sometimes it is deception. All the above is between each person and the Lord. But let us not throw the baby out with the bath water. Remember, I was eighteen years into the faith before that night in Tacoma and have lived over thirty more without as significant a replica. We can fake it, but if we are honest, we cannot make it happen. When Holy Spirit falls on us, it becomes a powerfully personal, loving moment impossible to forget.

Pastor Ed Glaspey of Restoration Ministries at Christ Center, Junction City, Oregon, tells the story of Holy Spirit "jumping" him while resting on his couch years ago. The experience was one of paralyzing and overwhelming ecstasy. Pastor Ed wondered if he would not die in the Lord's embrace. He was helpless and overcome by love. It was too much, as a human, for him to endure as he cried out for Jesus to release him. When the Lord relented, Pastor Ed was left exhausted but in a profound afterglow and, I will add, a marvelous testimony.

Explain away these experiences as you will, but if you are a Bible-believing Christian who walks with Holy Spirit, you cannot deny His participation in the lives of biblical personalities and historical figures, modern-day saints, and your own life. In reviewing your past, do not forget to include coincidence, karma, kismet, serendipity, chance, odds, luck, and breaks, which are simply the world's way of trying to take credit for Holy Spirit's intervention while giving credit where it is not due.

If that trip to Tacoma was a glorious Kiss from Heaven for ministers Susan and me, imagine how the trip that followed became a healing Kiss in Heaven for patient Susan.

QUESTION: What is the Kiss from Heaven in this God Story?

ANSWER: Few times in my Christian life have mirrored the early church like moments of worship, fellowship, and prayer while a part of host Susan's home group. During those days, an isolated Kitty Hawk moment and brief flight over fifteen feet of carpet in Casey Treat's Tacoma sanctuary, a crash landing in the lap of a Christian woman seated in the church's front row, and a sudden move to Benny Hinn's platform for an inebriated time of ministry always comes to mind. Wonderous as that Kiss from Heaven seemed, I am unaware of anything competing with our sister Susan's passing and longer but briefer flight early the following morning to the front row of Heaven, the open lap of Jesus, and no reason to move at all.

Eddie's Story (1997)

Tommy had been the first of Emily's thirteen siblings to lose his life and tragically to a land mine in Vietnam. Cliff had followed with pancreatic cancer, dying in the arms of Thelma, their mother. Years later, a call came from a family member sharing that Eddie, Emily's oldest surviving brother, had suffered a freakish accident on the sand dunes near Coos Bay, Oregon. It was 1997 when the throttle became stuck on Eddie's four-wheeler, carrying him airborne from a vertical sixty-foot dune. Eddie suffered severe head trauma upon impact, which eventually led to his premature death. Meanwhile, he spent months struggling to hold on to life in acute hospital care settings before discharge with little hope of recovery to a nursing home in Grants Pass. Emily and I were on our way to that facility to visit one Sunday afternoon with one of her younger brothers, Dennis.

After arriving, we asked at the information desk for Eddie's room number. Standing strategically near our side of the desk was a petite, well-dressed, elderly, silver-haired woman who joined us only after our business with the receptionist was complete. She instantly launched into an unsolicited message of the gospel as we walked the corridor toward Eddie's room. The old woman, holding fast as a Siamese twin, used a tiny book to illustrate her presentation with great spirit and conviction. Perilously dodging food carts, other Sunday visitors, and staff, our small contingent entered Eddie's room. Simultaneously, our companion, having finished her evangelical soliloquy, peeled off like a fighter jet, reversed course, and vanished.

Our attention focused so much on finding Eddie's room during the old woman's chatter that her message attracted little attention. Now, gathered with Emily and Dennis about my brother-in-law's bed, I took a moment to ponder our little evangelist's presentation. Her miniature book had five felt pages, each differing in color. She started with the green one, speaking of our being born into a lush and perfect world full of provision that God had created for us. Then, she continued, we had defiled it by our sin in the Garden of Eden, which she illustrated by flipping to the following black page.

Next, thumbing to the red one, she described how we were destined for and deserved just punishments for sin, which Jesus took upon Himself by shedding His blood as our substitute on the cross. Unstoppable, she presented the spotless white page portraying the cleansing we receive when accepting Christ into our lives, making us pure, holy, blameless, and beyond reproach in His eyes (Col.1:22). She beamed while flashing the final yellow one, that when we leave this earth, it will be to walk "streets of gold" with our Savior forever.

At that moment, I wondered if Eddie had ever been privy to that old woman's story. If so, being in such rough shape and unable to talk, would he have understood? After our visit, we doubted he could. Ending it in prayer, we slipped quietly from his room, expressing sadness over the futility of his suffering. He had been such a vibrant and energetic man, still very athletic and active into his fifties. As a stock car driver for years, it felt so unfitting for him to suffer defeat from a mere four-wheeler. Still, it was what it was and having had a three-wheeler partially disable me for more than a brief time, I understood how those risky ATVs had caused other unsuspecting riders much unexpected pain, disability, and, yes, even death.

Approaching the nursing home's exit, I glanced toward the front desk only to see a familiar face scurrying to close the distance between us. Our elderly silver-haired friend was laser-focused once more, determined, and refusing to be denied her quest. There was no opportunity for a polite exit and, for certain, she was not ready for us to deny her mission nor quench her zeal. Already into her message and effortlessly brandishing that little felt book, she flawlessly repeated her earlier evangelical witness verbatim. Looking around, I caught the eye of the volunteer working the desk and sensed both her sympathy for my plight and love for my "assailant." We waited patiently until our little gadfly for Jesus finished and returned to assume her strategic lookout at the receptionist's station. Seizing the opportunity before becoming total strangers to her again, we promptly hustled through the front door, looking over our shoulders until we gained the safety of our waiting car.

Postscript

Our most carefully planned endeavors often meet with detours, interruptions, interventions, or intercepts which, if we consider their purposes, often reveal the Lord quietly leading us into hidden opportunities beneath obvious surface realities. Bumping into that sweet elderly woman evangelist was not an accident but a heavenly intercept, and visiting Eddie was but a part of that day's purpose. Without even asking Jesus to show me, the answer became clear: Just because Eddie was brain-damaged and paralyzed did not mean God did not have an ongoing plan for his life. Would any of us that day have believed in advance that an elderly woman with significant Alzheimer's disease could function with such clever industry, inspiration, and knowledge? Considering Eddie's plight from the same perspective, I concluded despite what the future looked like from the world's eyes for Emily's prodigal brother, it was not over for Eddie until the Lord said it was over. After what Jesus revealed by using that elderly woman, we puzzled over what God might have in store for Emily's desperately disabled brother.

It was not long before the answer to that question came along. Eddie was making minimal but definite progress and occasionally speaking when he inexplicably failed quietly and then slipped away without fanfare. That might have been the sum of his sad story, making his accident pointless and another senseless tragedy. If not for the unrecognized, that would have left Eddie's life unfinished as a dangling participle.

But God had a Kiss from Heaven for this previously worldly, tough-minded, speed-demon of a man. Becoming alert enough toward the end of his life to recognize his future in question, Eddie invested his final days elsewhere. During one of Emily's visits, she and two of her sisters gathered about their brother's wheelchair while Emily spoke by the Spirit and with the same simplicity and clarity as that old woman evangelist, encouraging Eddie to consider what eternity held for him. A pragmatic man, her brother was not one to ignore his options. It seemed good to him to choose the one Emily presented, and so, over the next moments, Eddie received Christ into his heart to enter an eternal relationship with his Savior. Kiss from Heaven complete.

Outside the Lord and all of Heaven, I could imagine no one being happier on earth at that moment (aside from Eddie and the rest of us) than that silver-haired elderly woman evangelist with advancing Alzheimer's disease had she been present and not waiting expectantly at her assigned post in the lobby. It also presented an epiphany: Maybe our conclusions about Eddie's contact with that old gal were premature. If she twice shared her message with us in the space of one hour's time, how often outside visiting hours during the closing months of Eddie's life had she quietly slipped into his room to share her little felt booklet to help the Lord ready the fallow ground of Eddie's heart to receive Emily's salvation message when the time was right? Having seen that little evangelist's anointing, bulldog tenacity, and gift of forgetfulness, my guess (but a highly educated one it is) would be more times than enough.

Oh, I would have despaired had I not known that I would see the goodness of God in the land of the living (Ps. 27:13). Sometimes, all it takes is lookin' a little harder, doesn't it?

QUESTION: What is the Kiss from Heaven in this God Story?

ANSWER: Take an elderly woman with end-stage Alzheimer's disease, mix it with an older, unsaved, severely brain-injured nursing home resident, add a generous sprinkling of ministry from the old guy's sisters in love with Jesus, stir in a double portion of encouragement from that ever-present cloud of witnesses, and follow with the gospel of Jesus Christ. Then, add a pinch of the Sinner's Prayer, simmer for a moment, wait for a miracle, and then rejoice with the angels as hell loses another one to Heaven as Eddie, today's saved sinner, entered into the presence of Jesus as a child of God.*

Welcome home, Eddie. Save us a seat, brother.

*Aren't we overjoyed that the Lord is an equal-opportunity employer?

ESPN (1996/2007)

Emily and I traveled the Northwest extensively in the mid-nineties during weekends, seeking a large diesel-powered trawler to cruise the inland passageway to Alaska when we retired. In due course, our extended journey took us throughout Oregon, Washington State, and British Columbia. One particularly rainy gray northwest day, our trip ended on the northern tip of the Olympic Peninsula beneath fog-shrouded Hurricane Ridge in the smallish town of Sequim, inspecting an elderly but pristine wooden Chris Craft inboard.

Her equally venerable and longtime owner was lovingly touting her finer attributes when he curiously paused in mid-sentence. In a word search, he looked aloft, paused, and said, "Give it to me now." Emily and I caught one another's eye. At once, the old fellow continued with his infomercial only to mire down in confusing details that prompted him to again pause, look toward Heaven and implore, "Give it to me now." Again, Emily and I exchanged a glance. Jumpstarted, the old man continued his presentation, often repeating his word search all the way to a marathon finish. Afterward, we thanked him and went our way.

His cognitive disorder, though mild, needed tuning. Most understand that in the preliminary stages when memory fails, a person often equivocates to fill in the holes. (Lie is a hard description to use because it implies an intent to deceive.) This process, seeming benign at the outset, snares us with unintended consequences, which may find our minds bogged down in confusion and fiction. What starts as an innocent way to mask a gradual loss of memory or word retrieval results in a willful self-deception.

Now, I am not condemning the process nor judging its users. It is a common unintended path humans take. Instead, I wish to deal with an alternative. Our friend on the Olympic Peninsula seemed an honest man who treasured the truth and was unwilling to bend it. His intent was not a word search to fill in the blanks but to seek truth. Instead of depending on his faltering mind to come up with the answers, he would instead ask Holy Spirit for help. "Give it to me now" was his consistent petition and road to each solution. And, sure enough, time after time, the Lord would supply him with an answer. Now, his "memory road," populated with potholes, required multiple requests for the Spirit to fill voids before moving on. Here is my point: Though unsteadily, the old man progressed in truth to keep his integrity.

When Jesus said, "Without me you can do nothing" (John 15:5b), we often think of the Lord covertly directing our paths, inwardly empowering us, or privately enlightening our minds with deeper understanding. Walking with Jesus seems to imply that He is silently helping us in our efforts. All that is true. But couldn't this be as true: When handicapped (as in the old man's case with failed thought processes devoted to the truth), might our weakness then let Jesus work even more publicly, responsively, and effectively in our lives as we become more visibly dependent upon Him? Might that mean He becomes more tangibly involved in our day-to-day living as we become more reliant? Might entire dependence finally result in manifesting the mind of Christ alone if we follow the old man's path step-by-step? Then, consider the testimony.

Now I hear the grumblings and accusations of being out of touch with reality, that progressive mental decline is a hallmark of neurological aging, and that neurodegenerative disease is a fact. That is true. However, if our God is the God of impossibilities, then who is limiting Him in this age of ravaging dementia other than those living in unbelief about His power to heal and ignoring His commandment to minister healing? All I am proposing is that we have again given up while embroiled in yet another worldly dilemma that offers an otherworldly solution. If Jesus commanded us to heal the sick and raise the dead, and we are not doing so, how much more possible is it for someone with a cognitive disorder to languish because no one is praying or obeying? A mere question, but a good one.

We did not buy our elderly gentleman's pride and joy, which I sensed was a relief. Nor, sadly enough, did we pray for him. Regrettably, I am uncertain where he ended up. Progressive dementia can be problematic for anyone in its grasp. If, over time, he "lost his mind," I suspect he was not burdened by confusion, equivocation, and fabrication. His few remaining memories? I hope they were nuggets of preserved truth and that, moment by moment, he continued to rely on the mind of Christ ("Give it to me now, Holy Spirit, give it to me now"), followed by one revealed word at a time, each met with gratitude as one Kiss from Heaven after another.

Postscript

One mid-morning in August 2007, I was at my computer making little progress on this project when, out of nowhere, a thought popped up that we needed to get together for a meal with my nephew and his wife. The previous week, I had spoken with both, and each was agreeable. Intending to broach this subject with Emily over today's brunch, within seconds, the phone rang. It was my nephew's wife. She wondered if we could get together for supper that weekend. Sharing my similar and still-fresh thoughts, we laughed. "ESPN," she continued to chuckle, "just ESPN."

"ESPN," the Extra-Sensory Perception Network. That is cute. Although humorous, this is but one way to explain away events like today's inexplicably prompted phone call from my nephew's wife. Folks often rely on coincidence, serendipity, karma, kismet, chance, luck, or something akin when forced to explain the inexplicable. Edging out Holy Spirit by obscuring His reality with rational or irrational counterfeits may satisfy surface curiosities and conundrums, but, unfortunately, it will always avoid the deeper issue. What is that?

Well, when we prohibit Holy Spirit from preparing our lives for the day when we are no longer able (like our friend in Sequim) to function without help, where will we confidently turn when we are no longer self-reliant, when our memory accounts are empty, and our relationships are exhausted? To whom will we plead, "Give it to me now," and confidently depend for a satisfactory answer? Not "ESPN." In such instances, an explanation from an intangible source will never do; truthfully, we will need a Kiss from Heaven from a real person. Jesus said, "I will never leave you, nor will I forsake you" (Heb. 13:5). Tell me, has "ESPN" ever told you that?

Acknowledging that Jesus can simultaneously communicate with over two billion five hundred million Christians mystifies us. That He can do so in 6,912 languages with 39,491 dialects leaves us speechless. Doing this with high-maintenance dementia patients challenged to follow the simplest of computations, tasks, or conversations leaves us awestruck. Then again, considering that Jesus has not only given names and addresses to each of the two hundred billion trillion stars in His heavens (Ps. 147:4) while tracking their activities as they move through our universe at 124,000,000 miles per hour (Isa. 40:26), what is it to take on a mere two-billion-plus added conversations in thousands of languages and dialects to Him? Trifling? Yes. Unimportant? No.

In our earlier meeting with the elderly boat owner on the northern tip of the Olympic Peninsula, the King of Kings and Lord of Lords patiently devoted His full attention to helping one elderly dementia patient (approaching fifty-five million worldwide) struggling to ferret out forgotten details about an equally aged but treasured little wooden boat. Need I go on? What a loving, merciful, compassionate, understanding, and unhurried Father we are privileged to depend on for the most ordinary of needs, especially when we can no longer count upon ourselves.

As if we ever could (John 15:5b).

QUESTION: What is the Kiss from Heaven in this God Story?

ANSWER: This tale started over twenty-five years ago at a time when Caleb was already losing his glasses and car keys at work. Well, the only change to that scenario is . . . I am no longer employed. You should know, however, that years ago, I adopted that old man's method of retrieving glasses, keys, words, names, and places. "Give it to me now, Lord, give it to me now," has become my go-to method. Confidentially, I frequently default to my Emily for backup when the Lord seems busy.

The Swede (1998)

The Pensacola Outpouring (Brownsville Revival), from 1995 to 2000, despite its vocal critics at the time and all the dog-piling naysayers after the fact, was, in the truest sense, an American Christian revival that basked in the "thrills of victory" but perished, like scores of its predecessors, in the "agonies of defeat." Prophesied through God's man, the late David Yonge Cho of South Korea (at one time pastor of the world's largest church) and birthed by Holy Spirit in the hungry hearts of Pastor John Kilpatrick, Dick Ruben, and Lila Terhune's intercessors, the revival thrived under Spirit-led Evangelist Steven Hill, Teacher Michael Brown, and Pastor Kilpatrick himself only to succumb beneath the thumbprints of self-appointed, politically driven, and fiscally inept men. So, this revival rejoiced in and struggled beneath the same delights and burdens of earlier revivals and sadly, too soon, found itself retired to the unsure voices of second-string Monday morning quarterbacks, hashing out the whys and wherefores of its demise with twenty-twenty hindsight.

Had Emily and I experienced but one night's meeting (we were actually there for forty-seven, but who's counting) with the opportunity to watch thousands of desperate seekers (prostitutes, playboy bunnies, drug addicts, pastors, priests, police, professional criminals, military people, athletes, witches, teenagers, lawyers, deacons, elders, children, octogenarians, students, murderers, rapists, journalists, doctors, television reporters, photographers, pimps, plumbers, electricians, and on and on) find peace with Christ, that one meeting would have been enough to convince us: Only Jesus Himself could have prophesied, birthed, conducted, and terminated this grand event. Truth known, no man was ever born gifted enough nor any devil able enough (let alone willing to stick his neck out) to create, manage, and conclude this grand enigma.

Yet the Lord works through the agency of fallen man, knowing full well his proven penchant for spiritual fatigue in the face of prolonged glory and the undaunted craving of his flesh to control destiny by himself. It eventually comes down to old Galatian tapes replaying themselves, beginning in the Spirit and ending in the flesh. What results are revivals with men striving to wrestle away from God or each other power, influence, status, riches, real estate, or fame He never designed a man to carry. So, the rock-solid Pensacola Outpouring gradually devolved, as had similar former moves of our infinite God, onto the slippery slopes of finite men and so met its inevitable end in those sinking sands. And yet, we are sure it was all in God's perfect timing and according to His predestined plan.

Did it surprise God? No. Could He see it coming? Certainly. It was His grand event. Should we be surprised, critical, or angry at the perpetrators of the endpoint? Why? Considering our human condition, it was a great run. Christians usually do the best they can until they can't. Men wear out. That is why God gives them grace up front and mercy following. Why, then, shouldn't we?

When it is all said and done, the solution to the whole Pensacola enigma ironically lies in the oft-repeated vernacular of Brownsville's one and only evangelist, the late Stephen Hill, "You need to get over it." But, please, do not stop there. Press on to ask these important questions: "Where are you now, God? Where may we meet again after Brownsville that we might join you in your glory?"

Meeting the Swede

The Swede was a people magnet, a tall, slender man who drew everyone's attention. Highlighted by his distinctly European-style skinny-legged trousers coming to a screeching halt four or five inches above a pair of pointy-toed black leather low-cut boots, he looked like a modern-day Ichabod Crane as he "gangled" his way about the revival. The most often-circulated story about the Swede was that he had worked his way from the continent as a seaman aboard a cargo vessel and eventually planned to continue through the states, Mexico, and further south into Central America by the summer of 1998. He kept his mission in life close to his vest, but everyone suspected that he was an evangelist of sorts. Undeniably, he carried an anointing. Waiting in "line" for entry into each evening's meeting was an up close and personal global Christian-o-rama. Six to eight people wide and stretching city blocks deep by the end of the afternoon, the line included believers from all over the planet. It was that line, as much as the revival meetings themselves, that held the true Brownsville experience. Here, Holy Spirit ministered in prayer, song, "good works," and occasional attesting miracles from early morning until evening when the sanctuary doors opened. Jesus healed broken hearts in that "line" by way of unscheduled divine intercepts with His unsuspecting children. Every day was a new adventure where we never knew what to expect.

Lingering in line early one unseasonably cool evening, I questioned Emily as to whether I needed a haircut. With hair lapping at my collar, what could she say? So, we placed this chore on our next day's "to-do" list. At that precise moment, who but the Swede came "gangling" his way down the line? Watching this peculiar man with his grand anointing was always intriguing. This afternoon, he caught me in the act; our eyes met, and at once, he made a beeline in our direction. "Uh, oh," I muttered under my breath, "Uh, oh. Busted!"

Wasting no time, he launched off in English, richly basted with a gooey Swedish accent, "Woood yuuu l-eye-k eh herercoot (Would you like a haircut)?" Emily and I exchanged smiles and nodded as if to say, "Looks like Holy Spirit is at it again." I felt like a powerless little child ushered to the principal's office as the Swede ceremoniously took my arm, firmly escorting me off the curb and a half-dozen steps into the adjacent parking lot. Racing, my mind questioned, "Did he want me to make an appointment? Was the van parked just feet away used as his place to cut hair?" En route, I struggled to make sense of this unfolding scenario with a little small talk, "Have you been cutting hair long?"

Expecting an answer in the affirmative, "Nooo," Swede replied.

"Well, how long," I pressed on, "have you been a barber?"

"A barber? No, I am not a barber," he countered amiably.

Uh, oh, I thought again (suppressing a small but distinctly cold shiver moving up my spine), *what have I gotten into*? Holy Spirit said something about going with the flow and that my hair would grow back. How comforting coming from Someone with no hair!

By now, hundreds of eyes, Emily's among them, focused on our unfolding parking lot tête-à-tête. Shifting focus back to the Swede, I caught him athletically warming up a pair of barber shears in one hand and waving his comb like a maestro's wand with the other. "OK," I sighed with high resignation, "it must be showtime."

Quick as a whistle, the Swede grabbed a fistful of hair trespassing upon my collar and recklessly severed it, "Keyrunch!" From the corner of my eye, I caught the victim parachuting lazily to the pavement, quickly followed in rapid succession by scores of other unsuspecting casualties. For an unknown reason, my mind flew to the not-altogether successful airborne support for the invasion at Normandy in WWII.

Clippity-clippity, clip-clip; hair was merrily parachuting everywhere at once while I stood paralyzed, trying to suppress the feeling of being prey in the grip of a predator. Mercifully out of my earshot but within the earshot of the crowd, Emily was busy denying that we even knew this man. With Emily's comment came an audible crescendo, "Ohhhhooooh," from the crowd, which, I add, was well within my earshot and falling to earth alongside my reliably good hair. Clippity-clip, Clippity-clip asserted those busy, determined, and unrelenting shears rhythmically breaking the silence of the now-muted crowd.

In a scant three to four more minutes, each more like an eternity, the Swede signaled the completion of his mission by pocketing his tools and picking up the collateral damage scattered about my feet. While I was silently questioning whether "quick" was a good thing with haircuts, I recalled my Marine boot camp experience, which was not. Then there was the Swede, after receiving my permission, praying for me, and refusing "wages," which he deferred to the night's offering. Then, picking up where he left off, away he "gangled" toward the end of the "line." I knew better than to ask this man of God if he wanted to take "cuts."

After slipping back into welcomed anonymity, Emily was quick to point out, "That is one of the most professional-looking haircuts you have ever been given." One thing was certain—it had been one of the most peculiar.

Five Nights of Penance

Nights later, we were waiting with the special anticipation that preceded every evening's meeting. Emily and I could not get enough of this revival. Our first week seemed more like a well-orchestrated weekend retreat than the experience both of us had enjoyed at the Toronto Blessing. There, the renewal felt more like a hospital, gentle and filled with God's healing love; here, the revival felt more like a boot camp. That was OK, I reminded myself; this "old" Marine could handle it.

Concluding each service, Stephen Hill, the evangelist, who I had felt a little heavy-handed, would offer a salvation call followed by a request for people who were "away from Jesus" to repent and come forward to get "right with God." For an entire week, I had watched this nightly drama unfold with no inclination to go to the altar. In total agreement it was important for others, I had also commented to Emily that I hoped we could just "get to the prayer," a time following service when the leaders of the revival would lay hands upon each saint willing to come forward. As far as I could see, Emily and I had taken care of all that repentance stuff in Toronto.

One evening, awaiting the invitation to end so we could get to prayer, the Lord spoke, "Get down to the front; I need to deal with you." Then, He clarified what He intended to address. Sheepishly and tardy for the invitation, I slunk down toward the small city of genuinely repenting humanity. Finding an inconspicuous place on its periphery, Jesus confronted my sin of the moment, convicted me of it, and then mercifully led me from godly remorse to repentance and forgiveness. Before ending the "session," the Lord shared what we would address the following night. This routine continued over the ensuing four evenings.

When my "season of repentance" was over, Holy Spirit let me remain seated while others came forward. Those times of getting right with God, however, after my five nights "down front," were never to be the same again. Jesus had changed my heart; watching folks find Christ or return to the fold had unexpectedly soared to become my most eagerly embraced and precious time of revival.

Meeting the Swede II

Having but ten minutes to spare before one evening's service, I hurried from the sanctuary in search of the men's restroom then uncharacteristically empty. Opening the door to a stall, I met with the most-unsightly scene imaginable; here was a toilet bowl smeared with feces in and out, filled with paper, clogged with elimination, and, of all things, a pair of irredeemably soiled undershorts. Making matters worse, this carnage had spilled onto the floor, resulting in more stool, paper, and contaminated water surrounding the commode. Oh, I could not recall seeing the likes of this mess in my life; it felt intentional, like the work of vandals. Frozen, Holy Spirit impressed me to police the area. Taking a small step into the stall, I reasoned, "If I spend time here, I will interrupt the service on my return; besides, they pay staff to do this kind of work." Ignoring the unction, I closed the stall's door and entered its companion for the "disabled." Poignant, wouldn't you say?

The taller commode was not a great vantage point; however, from it, I saw for a short distance beneath the stall's partition. When the next patron entered the men's room, he headed directly to that soiled, unoccupied stall, opened the door, and paused, as had I, for a moment. Still experiencing the revulsion, I knew he was feeling the same. Prepared to leave my commode to his use, before I had the chance to vacate, he moved across the restroom floor to pull a supply of paper towels from the wall dispenser. Proceeding back to the vacant stall, he began his vile work.

Conviction poured over me. First, I heard the underwear removed from the bowl and deposited into a nearby waste bin (more conviction). Then, paper towels swished around the bowl and floor (much more conviction). Finally, more towels along with bowl flushing after flushing (conviction laced with shame).

Curiously, when the man had completed his chore, he did not use the facility himself but simply washed up and left the restroom. Having passed by my vantage point successively during his labors, I had only seen legs clothed in tight-skinny-legged trousers that ended four to five inches above a pair of pointy-toed black leather low-cut boots. We both recognize the one who cleaned up that foul mess for Holy Spirit I had refused as no other but the Swede himself.

Another Night of Penance

Atop my throne, late for service because I had been too humiliated to leave before the Swede had completed his task, my shame neared paralysis. Sick to my stomach, the sorrow and grief in my spirit was unparalleled. Over missing my opportunity, I was broken. Jesus had given me a test, and I had failed. So, the Lord had summoned His servant, the Swede, who came instantly, obeyed His Master, and returned to the meeting minutes before I completed my visit. The Swede had never intended to use the restroom. He had simply been "on call" for Jesus, who conveniently defaulted to him when I was a "no-show." As much as at any other time in my life, I was crushed and filled with remorse over my clear unwillingness to follow Holy Spirit's leading. Oh, I had wanted to ask, "Lord, what's the big deal? It's a dirty restroom and not the holocaust." Saving my breath, I had known; I had clearly known. It was not the task; it was my disobedience.

But now, I did not know what to say or do. I agonized over my pride. I agonized over the reality of my malingering in the face of Swede's faithfulness. I agonized over the missed opportunity to bless those serving in the revival. I agonized over squandering a chance to bless Jesus that would never come again. I agonized over my lost season to sow seeds into the will of the Father. I agonized over my depraved, selfish, irreverently disrespectful, and rebellious state. I agonized because I saw myself for who I was and who I was not. Stripped of dignity and self-respect, imprisoned in that little enclosure by shame, guilt, sorrow, and grief, I knew that I would never forget this lesson about the humility, surrender, and obedience that Jesus needed of me nor how He had penetrated my heart with that truth by using a few moments from the yielded life of a nameless man we called the "Swede." Suddenly, I recognized exactly how to deal with all this pain.

Tonight, I would take a trip to the altar to carry my conviction and remorse all the way to repentance and find my Lord's forgiveness; then, I would be set free. Those earlier five evenings "down front" had taught me a thing or two. Returning to the sanctuary, I could hardly wait for all the worship and preaching to end to get to that invitation. Need I tell you, that night at the altar, Jesus and I had one swell time.

Postscript

It was not long before the Swede was no longer a fixture at our nightly meetings. His departure approached a personal loss for us; we owed him an unspoken debt of gratitude for the Kisses from Heaven he brought into our lives. Like so many, we assumed that the Lord's season of work for him in Pensacola with people like us was over and that he had headed toward Central America as rumored. Those were unconfirmed assumptions because, sadly, neither of us ever saw the Swede again.

Ever notice how Jesus sets us up? Let us see: First, there I was with my puffed-up self-assured sense of self-righteousness, which required Holy Spirit to kidnap me for five consecutive "down front" training sessions of enforced repentance for unrecognized (at least by me) character issues. Looking back, those sessions may have been preparation for yet another round, this time staged in the living laboratory of a lavatory, to put more of my self-inflated persona on display. How did the Lord fit Swede into the process? Beginning with this peculiar foreigner's kindness to draw my attention by way of a free haircut,

Jesus later used him to contrast my deliberate sloth with his willing obedience. It appears as if Jesus has an ongoing interest in our character and will go to great lengths to quietly unearth, address, and then correct our ingrained faults and weaknesses, doesn't it? Why? Simple. Character is foundational and must bear the weight of any anointing He wishes to give His servants.

Want to go further with the Lord? Learn not to hurt but to help others. That was Christianity 101 for the Swede. One of the most hazardous and potentially destructive Christians (one of which we should always be wary of but ready to help and restore) is a saint imbued with heavy anointing but saddled with weak character. Historically, we have seen this tragic tandem too often in the body of Christ; far too many names flood our thoughts, our own among them, if we are honest. Would we pay heed to correcting our own character deficits before being released into ministry, there would be fewer sheep in the body wounded or driven off by the anointed but still wounded "wolves" in our church leadership. Before you take offense at my characterizations here, wasn't Saul a raging, furious murderer-turned-apostle taken under tutelage by the Holy Spirit in Arabia (modern-day Jordan), later Damascus, Jerusalem, and beyond for years before God sent Barnabas to fetch him from Tarsus to Antioch and further growth among his brethren? Only later was he sent forth prepared by Holy Spirit, still under Barnabas's influence, and that not without incident, if we recall (Acts 15:37–40). Character, we see, is not a one-time growth event.

Regretfully, so many of our church shepherds, responsible for the sheep's care (nurture and protection), are not only needy and damaged themselves but, incredulous as it sounds, reluctant or refuse to set an example by pursuing and receiving ongoing ministry, mentoring, and discipleship surrounding their own inner deficiencies. Death and taxes are not the only inevitabilities, dear ones. Here is another.

Wounded people wound people. It is inevitable, a fact in the world and not a minor problem in the Church. Look, charisma does not define character. Knowledge does not define character. Talent does not define character. Gifting does not define character. Power does not define character. Position does not define character. Anointing does not define character. Confusing personality, pride, position, power, fame, or fortune for character in their leaders has sadly led sheep into ill-advised trust, leading to betrayal, emotional pain, disillusionment, and eventually backsliding. That will commonly come from unwise or unmitigated use of God-given authority by church leadership with tainted character. And who might that be? Do we all have a mirror handy?

Can we see why Jesus needed on-the-job training, intimate discipleship, and servanthood from His disciples before He sent them out? Then, as the pièce de résistance, He had them tarry for Holy Spirit, who alone could further empower them to prove the will of the Father. Wouldn't it have been something special to watch Peter, a defeated man, wanted criminal, coward in hiding, and a man ready to go back to fishing and quit the whole Jesus thing changed in the twinkling of an eye? Oh, to have been there when the Spirit fulfilled Jesus' prophecy of Peter becoming that rock, suddenly transformed with power from on high, and then preaching with the tongues of men and angels to see three thousand saved and the Church founded. Populating the Church with saints transformed by the Spirit like Peter, thankful sinners saved by grace, bathed in mercy, and clothed with power from on high are those intended to be the stewards overseeing Father's kingdom. As shepherds selflessly tending the King's flock and humble servants devoted to ministering in the Spirit to the King of Kings, Lord of Lords, servant leaders are to yield in humble obedience, always listening, then hearing, and finally following the directives, commands, and guidance of Holy Spirit as He personifies Christ our King, the head of the Church on Earth.

Can we find Waldo, the traditional modern-day church staffer in Western Christianity, routinely manifesting the above character traits? Or the rest of us? Not being critical, saint, just honest. And remember, it took but one thorn in his paw for the lion to require help, one degree off course crossing the Pacific Ocean to miss a port by hundreds of miles, and but one of Mrs. O'Leary's cows to ignite and burn down Chicago. Unexpected and unattended trivial things can change our worlds. It is easy to overlook the obvious and become a victim unless we are plugged into Holy Spirit and His ministry 24/7.

Meanwhile, the Spirit and the rest of us face a holy challenge. Do not merely take my word for it, saint. Rather, let Holy Spirit own your life and let the Swede show what it means to be His disciple. How might you recognize the man? Just look for European-style skinny-legged trousers and pointy-toed black leather low-cut boots. Trust me, they are the real giveaway. When you find him, be ready to receive your own, be it humbling, Kiss from Heaven. Maybe more than one.

QUESTION: What is the Kiss from Heaven in this God Story?

ANSWER: Has the Lord ever loved you so much to intentionally place another human in your life to pull you from your throne? (Sorry for the pun.) How is that? Well, He introduces you to an anointed, humble servant who looks, talks, acts, and treats you like Jesus. Then He turns around and uses that model human to humble (or humiliate) you to brokenness so you can see who you are and see who you aren't. It's kind of like being run over by a truck in a good way.

Then He draws you to Himself to patch and love you back to wholeness. Admittedly, it is a backhanded Kiss from Heaven, but I will testify a highly effective one. So, since "all things work together for good for those who love God and are called according to His purposes" (Rom. 8:28), I guess this bad boy God Story gets to stay on our kisses list. I once watched a killer whale in the waters off Juneau, Alaska, powerfully slapping its tail against the water thirteen times in a row to shed its barnacles. A reasonable analogy, don't you think? Well, except for the Lord doing the tail slapping.

Two One-Dollar Bills (1998)

What my father did, he did well, not compulsively but with ease. Paced but not driven, he thought everything through and then executed his plans to perfection. He was the most skilled trout fisherman since Isaac Walton, dropped each surprised partridge with his first shot, kept the most meticulous yard in the neighborhood, dressed like an Armani model, built everything with the precision of a Swiss watchmaker, conducted his business with the integrity of Gandhi, told the unvarnished truth like George Washington, was strong as Bunyan's ox, dashing as Errol Flynn, and, among other extras, self-controlled, kind, considerate, careful, and flat-out neighborly. And yes, in his youth he had earned his Eagle Scout. Unfortunately, all that was problematic because I had few of his qualities, at least in abundance.

That made life enigmatic in that while I longed to be like my dad and wished to please him at every turn, my natural bent was to contradict who he was. What a shattering disappointment for a youngster to never fit the mold and for parents to have such a recalcitrant child. Where my father was concerned, I was carefree. Where he was a perfectionist, I embodied "that's good enough for government work." Where he was restrained, I was demonstrative. Where he was a realist,

I was a dreamer. Where he was measured, I was impulsive. Where he tolerated, I loved (or took animus). Where he was a believer, I was a cynic. You get my drift, don't you.

The End of an Era

On March 13, 1985, my father passed away to be with our Lord. He had been living his latter days in Upstate New York as a widower while I was building a medical practice in Oregon as a doctor. During a counseling session (guess who was the counselee), I received a phone call that Dad had little time left. Without packing even so much as a toothbrush, I boarded the next flight to Syracuse, New York, to beat the grim reaper to his appointed rounds. Arriving at the hospital, I found my dad alert, comfortable, and upbeat while I, characteristically, had become befuddled, anxious, and depressed over the whole scenario. Discovering him confined to the hospital for two weeks while choosing not to let me know ("He didn't want to worry you, brother," explained my ever-present elder male sibling) was just another in a long line of metaphorical coffin nails in the relationship between my father and myself. Our only bedside conversation went this way: "How are you, son?" he asked. "Better than you, I think, Dad," was my tongue-tied retort. That was it; later that afternoon, I watched my father close his eyes and go to sleep for the final time.

Not ironically, he died in a room among a small city of teary-eyed nurses, nurses' aides, interns, and patients from various rooms on the floor expressing their condolences and voicing their enduring admiration for him. He had, as usual, endeared himself to everyone in a matter of days. Oh, how I obsessed over my having been walking around "fat, dumb, and happy" for the last two weeks while my father, unwilling to "trouble" me, was building and strengthening relationships with everyone else in Onondaga County. What else was new? We never seemed to connect, even to the last moment.

There were no tears because I rarely cry unless it is a waterfall. But I felt a loss and a numbness that betrayed deeper stuff going on. Dad's unwrinkled clothes were hanging neatly in his hospital closet, polished shoes lined up at attention, tie folded carefully so as not to crease, and wallet, change, and tie bar arranged in an orderly fashion on his shelf. Needing to touch and smell his personal effects, when left alone, I did so. Occasionally glancing toward the bed, I could see someone had carefully combed his hair and cleanly shaved his face as if he might spring forth from a power nap at any moment. It seemed so surreal, and I needed something of his to seal this moment, to give it real meaning, a memory with teeth. Taking his wallet, I removed a dollar bill, took a nearby pen, and scribbled the day's date over George Washington's face. Then I pocketed the "buck" and left the hospital. A couple of days later, after burying Dad next to Mom and alongside my sister and grandparents in Syracuse's Oakwood cemetery, the dated dollar bill—destined to snooze for the next thirteen years in my wallet—and I returned to Oregon and to life as usual.

A Painfully Inexpensive Sacrifice

One evening those thirteen years later, at the Brownsville Revival in Pensacola, Florida, Pastor John Kilpatrick's sidekick was asking us all to help support the meetings with a nightly offering. Emily and I contributed faithfully and as liberally as we could; this evening would be no exception. As I reached for my wallet, I heard the Lord say, "I want you to give Me the dollar bill." Oh, I knew His meaning, and it caused me to lose my breath. Audibly, I gasped. That request felt so uncalled for and insensitive. The Lord knew that I treasured that dollar bill with the date of my dad's death engraved upon George Washington's face as a precious reminder I came across daily; I could not let it go. It was such an unreasonable demand.

"Will you give that dollar bill to me, son? May I have it?" I seemed to hear the Lord say, softening His first request.

Please, Lord, don't make me do this, my thought countered.

"You don't have to give it to me," Holy Spirit spoke reassuringly, "but would you be willing to let it go?"

Oh, the struggle I went through. Did I say I rarely cry? Well, I cried a river that night both before and after I surrendered that bill to Heaven. It was so hard that today, decades after my dad's passing, I choke up revisiting that moment. Although I knew through my tears that the Lord had a purpose, I was unclear whether it was a passage or a test.

The Beginning of an Era

Weeks later, having left the Brownsville revival (Pensacola Outpouring) in body but not heart, Emily and I pulled into a mom-and-pop motel somewhere deep in Alabama. Returning from a late supper and prepared to enter our room for the night, I felt drawn to the motel's spacious front lawn. Something in its dimly lit center caught my eye, so excusing myself from a puzzled Emily, I made a beeline in that direction. Thirty feet away and perched atop the lawn's grassy fingers rested a spanking new crisp dollar bill. As I knelt to retrieve it, the Lord spoke, "Here you go, son; thanks for sharing your heart's treasure with Me in Pensacola. Keep this as a token, a reminder of how your Father in heaven loves and appreciates you."

It did not take rocket science to figure that out. My earthly father's dollar bill, reluctantly given up at the revival, had always engendered bittersweet emotion when I came across it in my wallet. How could it not? This fresh new specimen, I instantly understood, was given to remind me of my relationship with Abba, not bittersweet but always full of love and acceptance. "Thank you, Father," I happily confessed, "and I receive everything this token means to us from your heart." Whether that incident in Pensacola with Dad's dollar bill was a "test" must wait for Heaven. That it was a "passage" here on earth, when coupled with Abba's gift that evening in Alabama, however, was undeniable.

Postscript

How I am looking forward to meeting with my dad in Heaven to comfortably share Jesus's unconditional love. How I had longed for that relationship during our time together on this planet, but it had been hard. However, something inexplicable happened the night Father God gave me the crisp dollar bill. It was a signet time of transition where I seemed mysteriously reassigned to Heaven not only for Father's love and care but also for His molding and finishing. And what a perilous but wonderful and ever-unfinished journey through His workshop these intervening years have been.

Years later, while chatting over dinner with my dear wife, Emily, she looked across the table at me with love in her eyes and said, "You are a good man, Sweetie." Those words of admiration, love, and respect, uplifting in the ears of any husband, somehow filled a void I was not aware existed. Unknown to Emily and years before, my former wife had declared in a time of anger (and, more rightly than not), "You are a little man, Chuck (a nickname gradually losing ground)." In a flash, I saw the irony: By releasing my father to the Lord (giving Him that worn dollar) and entering a nurturing relationship with Father God (receiving that fresh new bill), a new work had begun. The qualities I had admired about my dad, for years antithetical to my own character, were gradually taking a foothold in my life.

My sweet wife's comment that evening, and but one Kiss from Heaven in this story, caused me to pause and ponder, "Lord, was my Emily's comment this evening meant to tell me that I have passed your test?" No immediate answer, but I would like to think Father was busy sharing a high five with Jesus. Realistically, we might wait awhile for future clarification on that somewhat less than humble thought . . . or longer.

QUESTION: Where is the Kiss from Heaven in this God Story?

ANSWER: Our Bible says that God is love and we love because God loved us. If we feel unlovable or find it difficult to love others, it is because we have difficulty receiving His love or passing it on. Why? Because it is impossible to receive love and pass it on when we believe and feel ourselves faulty, wrong, missing a link, unimportant, a failure, have a screw loose, not enough, unwanted, bad, worthless, guilty, shameful, stupid, ugly, dirty, and so on. Then, we cannot give away what we have never received.

Children traumatized often believe and feel themselves unlovable after assuming negative false identities based on neglect and abusive experiences. We should also note that love perceived during childhood trauma (e.g., a gentle caressing molestation by a pedophile) may unfortunately not be seen as trauma by a child, not create a negative identity, but regrettably lead to enjoying promiscuity to feel lovable as an adult. A true God-given identity, however, created by a healthy, loving parent throughout childhood will lead to a healthy love of God, self, and others despite occasional errors in discipline. Sometimes, a child's identity may be less decided by the severity of a traumatic experience than by how much the child feels loved by the one delivering it.

Was your discipline enforced by understanding authority figures who valued you enough to explain the reason for their balanced actions or by out-of-control adults reacting in cold rage, not equating their punishment to your behavior? Which of the above adult treatments bring a sense of value, and which one worthlessness? The truth is that children know when their correction is just, to what degree they are punished for innocence, and whether the discipline is done in love. The degree of perceived love will often overcome the perceived inequity of the punishment in shaping a child's identity.

Fortunately, full-blown negative false identities carried into adulthood by traumatized children are subject to change if the adults consent to let the Lord set them free from the lies they have believed as truth by bringing His truth to set them free. It is a victorious process but never a traumatic one. Emily and I are proof positive.

The Venezuelan Telegraph (2000)

It was the year of our Lord 2000 when I asked my corpulent body to prepare itself to climb the eastern foothills of the renowned Andes Mountains of northwestern Venezuela as part of a team assembled by our local church to search out an unreached native people group yet to hear the wonderful news of Jesus. Rising early each morning for three consecutive months in advance, I shouldered a backpack housing a twenty-five-pound weight to hike the steeper climbs west of Monroe, Oregon, for two intense hours. For young workout fanatics, those daily Oregon jaunts would hardly have been demanding, but for a dumpy, out-of-shape, sixty-year-old guy, it was a task of heroic proportions. Our leader lectured those South American mountains would be a daunting challenge for our "long-in-the-tooth" compatriots. Not every "long-toothed" team member heard that message.

Stark reality motivated my preparation. During former years, I had been a competitive athlete, combat Marine, and long-distance runner of sorts. Despite that history, I knew the only way to make those Venezuelan hills compatible with our team's general increase in aging and decreased conditioning was to either avoid the climb or rent a couple of Hannibal's elephants for the weekend.

Unfortunately, neither solution looked promising. An added personal incentive was to seek a level of fitness that would make me available to help one essential team member likely to struggle along the way. Our leader was a pastor of immeasurable drive and boundless energy who, regrettably, had a heart laced with bypasses and a bloodstream loaded with cardiac drugs. Being a doctor, I felt obliged, were it necessary, to help him around the crags, through the crevices, and over the precipices during our journey. Alas, well...let's press on.

The Journey Begins

From the outset, Pastor John Smith (not his actual name, but you knew that) was visibly out front, exhorting his struggling "over-the-hill gang" over the next hill. Then, in a flash, deftly repelling down the present mountainside to become our rear guard, he would be found encouraging the stragglers up ever-steepening inclines while shouldering pieces of their gear. I was, understandably, becoming concerned for him overdoing his heart's potential.

Burros (the locals were out of elephants) rented to transport duffels and supplies, themselves out of gas from carrying exhausted climbers, were soon being exhorted by our indefatigable pastor. Who was this man? The air was becoming progressively thinner and our path relentlessly more challenging when I suddenly realized that having fantasized this trek as another morning's stroll through the rolling hills and dales of Monroe was keeping me in significant denial, exhortations aside. So, as a good Marine, I faced this ugly reality: I needed to concentrate on keeping my breathing aerobic, the sweat from my eyes, and recommitting myself, step by onerous step, to packing my own overweight body and burdensome gear ever skyward. Then came a new reality. It was every man for himself.

All attempts to help others up the face of this K2-like monster rapidly faded into good intentions. What little spare time we were allotted for "breaks" I spent in newfound gratefulness to Jesus for keeping Pastor, bad heart and all, repetitively and vigorously pressing toward the summit while requiring none of my aid. As the likelihood of Pastor needing my services faded, there came a welcome epiphany: He was now available to help should I falter along the way. What a self-absorbed turn of events this journey had become!

Seeking redemption from my ballooning myopia, I helped a weary fellow traveler down an extended steep decline as we approached our destination. Depositing him gently onto a soft mattress of cool grass and into even deeper slumber, as a Good Samaritan wannabe, I slipped away. The temporary sense of altruism in the wake of that others-centered self-sacrifice soon faded a whole lot faster than the glory from Moses' face. No veil needed here as, by the following morning, a small army of tireless workers were busy laboring to pluck off hundreds of tiny grass ticks determined to hold fast to yesterday's Christian whom I had so selflessly "rescued."

Why should those ticks have given up easily, anyway? Our weary brother had been a once-in-a-lifetime opportunity, a defenseless McHuman found slumbering in the recesses of their own grassy bedrooms. Then, as if that quasi-medical exorcism of the ticks on foreign soil had not been enough, his unfortunate wife had the pleasure of plucking another three hundred of those annoying bloodsuckers from sundry body parts (to remain anonymous) upon his return home.

That clinical mishap gives perspective as to why my value as a preventive care doctor on that trip became suspect and may have been one of the more celebrated reasons for my failed induction into the "Venezuelan Good Samaritan Hall of Fame" had there been such an animal.

A Booming Message

The following day, we battle-weary folks forded a shallow stream in a small valley west of camp (where I had pitched my tent) before plunging into the thick jungle underbrush, heading toward our scheduled meeting with a native people group descending from the Andes highlands. Countless tentacles from philodendron plants dangling alongside other tropical species (often first cousins to those found in Wal-Mart nurseries stateside) from the dense canopy overhead cluttered our pathway. Swarms of parrots, tails streaming as multicolored contrails, complained noisily in their hasty retreats through those towering treetops while nervous monkeys scampered aloft, searching safety in that near-impervious foliage squeezing this morning's sun into a thousand points of light.

Trudging skyward for an hour, our valiant contingent of over-the-hill warriors finally made it over the hill by bursting onto a sun-drenched clearing a stone's throw from a group of surprised but curious locals. The translators from both groups were soon busily warming up their skills while leaders from each side became acquainted. Within minutes, it was all-hands-on-deck, the only semi-level patch of ground, it appeared, available on the mountainside. The scantily clad natives, having arrived earlier from higher climes, were sitting cross-legged in back-to-back rows while a pastor from Harlem, New York, an imposing African American with Big Bertha for a voice, without hesitation began to deliver an animated salvation message. Observing from a short distance, it troubled me to see a multiplying number of wide-eyed native faces appearing among the pastor's captive audience. And for good reason: A mere few feet from their front row, our preacher was bellowing at the top of his lungs, delivering repetitive gospel salvos toward those natives who, cringing at his point-blank delivery, were in a losing battle to recover their former placid demeanors. Confused, I could not fathom for one second why that pastor felt the need to holler with such blatant insensitivity into the faces of these gentle people. As time dragged on (and it did), I felt sympathy, then empathy (since I, too, was enduring this barrage), for those trapped natives and humiliation for, if not a mounting irritation with, that bombastic evangelist.

Oh my, then the message became not only interminable by requiring translation from English to Spanish and again from Spanish to the natives' dialect. Incessant periods of endless hollering, shouting, gesticulating, and leaping alternated with translation upon translation upon translation went on and on and on. Then, at long last, thank you, blessed and merciful Jesus, the preacher paused long enough to hold an altar call without an altar, which, in my humble opinion, was to be a vain and mortifying attempt to secure these lovely people for the kingdom. *No way, Jose*, I thought. *Who would want any part of this? Who among these lovely, gentle, shell-shocked, PTSD-eligible natives would ever want to serve such a noisy God?* Well, sheepishly, I admit, each one.

A Hearty But Soggy Conclusion

Exhausted and in need of a meal by that time, a little past 3:00 p.m., the day's feast stood ready for preparation. Well, let me rephrase that: We were ready, but it is highly unlikely that the "feast" herself was ready. With all the competence of a board-certified surgeon, one skillful native butcher selected a nanny scapegoat (whose quiet grazing beside the crude shelter where we were now gathered was rudely terminated), deftly nicked her carotid artery, hung her up by the hind legs to drain to a Maxwell House last drop, chopped the old girl into steaks and, as the pièce de résistance, flipped her filet by filet onto a blazing fire to await our, speaking for myself anyway, somewhat ambivalent palates. Nanny-meal ended (none too soon for me), and both sides bid fond farewells and went their separate ways.

Back to Base

The return journey retraced our inbound path, a simple task had it not been for the day's end, darkness, and the onset of a heavy tropical downpour. Refreshing, it was also obscuring our way through the suddenly blackened jungle. Approaching home base, we found the shallow stream easily crossed earlier that day had become a raging three feet of torrent navigable only by our Venezuelan "sherpas" stretching a heavy hemp rope from one overflowing riverbank to the other. Dutifully, each voyager gingerly forded the turbulent waist-deep water by holding ever-so-tightly to the rope and often one another. Frazzled, not one soul hesitated to head directly to the sleeping quarters. Industriously strung hammocks in the crude shelter on a knoll in plain but ominous sight of that infamous tick-infested grassy bed filled up quickly while others, me among them, sought their tents in the valley nearby the receding waters of the recently forded river. Who could forget the unrelenting high-pitch whines emanating from clouds of dive-bombing Kamikaze mosquito squadrons throughout that bug-infested night nor the early-morning monsoon-like torrent that found that nearby stream rising to where I soon found myself dog paddling about my tent looking for a place to dock. If anything was to be learned during that eight-hour holocaust, it was this: When a manufacturer couples the adjective "waterproof" to the noun "tent," you may be assured that porous piece of imperfection had never been subjected in advance to rigorous early-morning tent testing in a flooded Venezuelan valley.

A Divine Intercept

Fortunately, there had been a lull in the downpour between yesterday's return from our mountain outreach and the early-morning "swim" I took in my riverside tent. Another member of our expedition was not sleeping well. Rising from his hammock, he heard singing across the river where a remnant of our team had set up camp. Flashlight in hand, he worked his way across the again temporarily navigable water to join those folks where their small campfire, illuminating a small area forged from the surrounding darkness, was vainly trying to dry everyone's clothing while simultaneously struggling to warm the chilly night's air.

Suddenly, amid the singing, out of those shadows carved into the jungle by the campfire came two figures heading directly toward the surprised and instantly silenced worshippers. On guard, everyone was delighted to welcome two men when found friendly. The team members asked from where they had come and how they discovered tonight's remote location. When allowed, the men unwrapped a tale that would not only satisfy everyone's curiosity but eventually solve a lingering conundrum for yours truly and give greater glory to God.

From the Horse's Mouth

Approaching three o'clock in the afternoon, the two men had been walking through a valley, separated by an entire mountain range from that bellicose African American preacher assaulting Heaven and Earth on behalf of those cringing natives. Startling our visitors trekking miles away, that preacher's booming Big Bertha of a voice came rumbling like an avalanche through the mountain chain they were paralleling. The voice had gone on at length to describe this God, Jesus Christ, while pausing often enough for the men to confirm and discuss what they had heard. Intrigued, within minutes, they left their valley to cross the mountains (presumably through a pass) in search of that voice, now portraying a Savior who came to earth to suffer on a cross for humanity's sin as the only way to reconcile us to a personal love relationship with His Father.

Punctuated by extended periods of silence, the voice would continue, dwelling on the forgiveness that Father God promised all humankind, an abundant life filled with the joy of His presence that would follow, and, finally, His promise to never leave or forsake us if we believed in Jesus as our Lord and Savior. We would be His children, and He would be our Father, save us from sin, heal us from disease, and deliver us from dark spirits. The voice eventually stopped, but the men, now determined, did not. They pressed on to find the way to this God, Jesus. When finished with their animated story,* they paused long enough to ask if what they heard during their journey was true and, if so, could the folks surrounding the fire tonight introduce them to this Jesus. Willingly, the Christians gathered about their visitors, not only leading them to the Lord but praying for all their needs.

Postscript

Let us sum up this episode to seek clarity. Okay, here we were at three o'clock in the afternoon, a bunch of old rusty coots, mostly from Oregon, on a jungle mountainside in a different hemisphere, way out of our comfort zone, and preparing to preach to an unreached Venezuelan people group the gospel of the kingdom of Heaven. Unknown to any of us but known to Jesus, at the same moment, two lost souls were about to miss the entire event by wandering miles away on the far side of a nearby mountain range. Now, the Bible shares with us this truth: "The eyes of the Lord roam to and fro throughout the earth that He may support the hearts of those who are completely His" (2 Chr. 16:9). Happily for us, we met the Lord's criterion: We were completely His, the soon-saved native people group would be completely His, and the two guys wandering along the other side of the mountains were intended to be completely His.

Don't you suspect, as I do, that the Lord saw this dilemma develop during a time His eyes were roaming "to and fro," and, as is His fashion, He jumped in to help? We cannot be certain, but what followed may have gone like this: "Oops," Jesus chuckled, "there is always the 10 percent, two guys who did not get the word and will miss this afternoon's meeting. Let's straighten out this mistake. Hmmm, call the messenger angels (Heb. 1:14) to help carry Big Bertha's words over that mountain chain. Then let us arrange a meeting this evening between those two vagabonds and a bunch of those old rusty coots from Oregon."

So, as is His habit, Jesus left the ninety-nine (well, here the ninety-eight) to spin a creative miracle, assuring two lost souls from the far side of those mountains a place in His everlasting flock on our side. Aided by a loud-mouthed preacher, a Sermon-on-the-Mount-like setting, a whole lot of angel amplifiers, and a few Christian folks being drip-dried around a campfire that night, He delivered a whole bunch of Kisses from Heaven—not only to two hungry souls but to all He invited, some who crashed the party, and even, in absentia, the likes of me who was left off that night's invitation list. (Hey, how might you have felt when you missed that party?) At least it finally made sense why that imposing African American pastor with his booming Big Bertha voice was along for the ride. Conundrum solved.

*The preaching that cascaded over the mountains and heard by those two men was based on what I gleaned from the imposing African American pastor's presentation earlier that afternoon. I was, if you recall, little more than a puzzled eavesdropper at that ground-breaking event. And for good reason, it ended up.

QUESTION: Where is the Kiss from Heaven from this God Story?

ANSWER: No competition here. How that bombastic preacher's voice carried miles across that mountain range to those two English-speaking natives who not only heard that message in detail but made it through those mountains to a modest campfire in the dark of night could only have been by divine intervention. So glad we have messenger angels, aren't you? Even more so, a Jesus who never fails to tie up loose ends of what He begins.

Have you a few loose ends that need tying up, Christian? Well, get in line. We have not because we ask not.

♥ 15

My Brother's Passing (2003)

Do you remember yesteryear when the politically correct media treated each prospective Wal-Mart Supercenter like a budding pimple on the unblemished face of a virgin twelve-year-old? I mean this: First, they scrutinized it, then tried to squeeze it to death, and finally covered it up like it never happened. It all started with the rumor that the villainous Wal-Mart gang was on its way to plunder a small town's economy and ended up, after months of applied pressure to make it go away, in complete denial that the new store was keeping several scores of recently employed townsfolk from plunging beneath the federal poverty level, offered financially strapped citizen-shoppers affordable prices on everything from Grandpa Chad's bran flakes to Grandma Jennifer's arthritis pills and, believe it or not, stimulated other businesses in town to become lean, mean, competitive and, sometimes, more profitable than ever. (Do you remember dealing with this? If a former small business owner struggling in a dinky town, you do!) Okay, Pandora's Box is now open, so we can all begin a rant about children working in Wal-Mart's Myanmar supply chain for less than "minimum wage" (Do you honestly think Myanmar has a minimum wage?). Instead, shouldn't we thank Wal-Mart for keeping those kids alive with roofs over their heads and food on their tables? Hey, if not for Wal-Mart's workforce, they would be homeless and suffering from malnutrition. Next?

While we are at it, we might as well memorialize the infamous hordes of uncivilized Genghis Kahn "Barbarellas" (universally painted as victims of irresponsible corporate crowd control and drooling "ambulance chasing" lawyers), who reliably storm the gates during Wal-Mart's Black Friday sales events like crack WWII German panzer divisions apparently willing to crush offspring underfoot for a 25 percent savings on a water pick, plus-sized moo-moo, or Hannah Montana's latest rage (Okay, we are retro here to stay reminiscent in this story). As the Prophet Gump once said, "Stupid is as stupid does." Anymore, does anyone modify the noun "behavior" with the adjective "responsible"? Frankly, not much.

Do I sense derision arising from RV park industry campaigns to ban overnight RV parking in Wal-Mart stores? Maybe. Emily and I spent seven years in unpaid ministry as road warriors. When that journey ended, RV sites cost upward of forty dollars a night. Let us calculate a year's worth of that rent for you: $14,600 for a glorified sleepover in your own bed; let's not forget the extra $8,000 during those same twelve months for mortgage payments on your $200,000 house sitting vacant in your hometown. Senior kudos to Wal-Mart for allowing overnight privileges in designated parking areas to save older folks all that money. Add safety guaranteed by motorized security guards, available fast food, and shopping for necessities on your list, and how could we not offer thanks and loyalty to those traveler friendly superstores? As a finale, have you ever seen a larger quantity of "gray ghosts" kept out of the bread lines by any other single senior-friendly employer? Not yet, amigo; so, "viva" free enterprise.

A Visit to End All Visits

We were near the end of our sojourning in the snowy spring of 2003. Pulling into one of the Wal-Marts in Rochester, New York, Emily and I detached Ester (the tow car) to visit my only surviving sibling and brother in nearby Penfield. Bordering seventy-three and contending with heart disease for two decades, one mitral valve repair and two bypass surgeries later, he suffered another devastating event, a massive stroke. Affecting his motor skills less than mellowing his personality, my sister-in-law admitted it made him more relational and less intense. Reconciling this description with the brother I knew would take a little gear shifting. However, he confirmed her evaluation at our greeting; was I meeting a stranger? He stayed in his recliner while previously would be on his feet, smiling, shaking my hand, questioning our trip, and asking how we had been faring. Content and much more relaxed than usual, his wife was heartily enjoying this new journey, which, after forty years and five children, was finally offering her a chance to nurture this until now fiercely independent and close-to-the-vest male animal.

The following day, Emily and I were two hundred miles east of Rochester in a once economically vibrant small rural upstate town now showing the crippling signs of failed industry (empty stores, broken down mills, and skeleton factories) when my sister-in-law called. Suffering from abdominal pain, my brother was being rushed in an ambulance to a local hospital emergency room. We sped back to a busy, hectic, understaffed facility where patients on gurneys lined most corridors as hurried medical professionals bullied their way past one another, trying to manage a tide of new arrivals. Local police officers escorting a troubled youth thrust us aside as we reached my brother's cubicle.

Resting, he reluctantly admitted to having abdominal pain. Without a stethoscope, I pressed my ear to his firm, distended belly. I noticed rebound tenderness. Then, there were no bowel sounds. That meant trouble. The nurse assigned relayed that the gastroenterologist on call sent a referral to a general surgeon who had yet to arrive. When he did, without hesitation, an orderly rushed my brother to an operating suite to repair a ruptured bowel. I thought, "The poor guy can't catch a break."

Someone once said, "The surgery was successful, but the patient died." That is an oxymoron to the lay public, but to doctors, it simply means that the technical part of the procedure went as scheduled, but the patient forgot to "cooperate" by not improving but regrettably passing. Well, my brother always cooperated; he was a skilled people person and a determined competitor. More than anything, he loved life. Sadly, in this case, his body betrayed both his zest for living and the surgeon's efforts to remedy a dreadful cardiac arrest, which mandated rapid wound closure midway through his case and a speedy trip to the ICU.

Already on the canvas, he suffered through a second arrest followed by the all-too-common shuffle that begins between surgical and medical services when the two share an "uncooperative" patient. Each discipline, after recognizing the gravity and failing condition of their charge and the extra work the charge demands, feels the other service is more suitable to assume care. That common tempest arising in such multidisciplined teapots often prophesies a poor outcome for any patient caught in its boil. Sure enough, my brother had a final event, a stroke that led to a coma. The neurologist, in less than a kind and gentle moment, declared him functionally "brain-dead," which clinically meant part of his brain, the brain stem, was still supporting essential functions like breathing and his heart beating, but the rest was no longer living and my brother not aware.

A Time to Ruminate

We now entered the period of palliative care where the nurses keep the patient "comfortable" while the family struggles to reach consensus between pitting the use of heroic measures to extend a gravely ill life and withdrawing all forms of life support to let the patient pass. There are often prolonged, wearying, and volatile family discussions and although a patient has enunciated wishes in advance through a durable power of attorney for health care or other legal documents, still well-intentioned and distraught family members commonly and understandably often try to dissuade the remaining folks from keeping the patient's wishes. And so, we embarked my brother upon the "road more or less traveled" by adding a little more "Miracle-Gro" to our nurse's watering cans. You know I would have been highly resistant to this course, although no more influential, if uncertain my brother was unaware of his surroundings.

As is usually the case, once the course was on autopilot, the vigils began. My valiant sister-in-law was unwavering about being at her husband's bedside when he passed, an unpredictable event as he was receiving fluids to promote comfort. She was both spending nights by his side and keeping watch by day. Soon, others would stand occasional duty in relief; I became the chosen guardian for the evening of July 7, 2003.

A Night to Remember

Propped up like a giant stuffed panda bear in the bed, deep in a coma, head slumped to one side, he had been recently equipped with an NG (nasogastric) tube entering its journey through a left nostril on an esophageal descent to evacuate the contents of his stomach. Endlessly running IV fluids, through due process, found their way into a catheter bag hung precariously from a bed rail. His breathing was remarkably comfortable for a patient who had aspirated an entire stomach's contents into an unsuspecting right lung the previous day, prompting remedial placement of that NG (nasogastric) tube.

This whole scenario was over the top and five weeks in the making. The guy had always been tougher than tripe and never a complainer. Even now, I knew, were he to regain consciousness, his first words would be, "You do not have to be here, brother. Go home and rest." That was my bottom-line caretaker-brother in a proverbial nutshell.

Origins

He was a "junior" named after my father. Cloning is not a recent phenomenon, friend; it appeared in our home in 1931. While the father and his firstborn son did not resemble one another physically early on, there ended the dissimilarities. Each bit of body language, voice intonation, chosen verbiage, meticulous way of dressing, serious demeanor, rigid belief system, consideration and respect for others, abstinence from critical or negative speech, kindness, and consistently cheerful outlook were mutually shared. They were both born leaders, endeared to their friends, loyal to their spouses and parents, faithful to their God, fiscally conservative, morally immovable, responsible to a fault, and especially good guys. They had both lived their lives as proud Americans, willing taxpayers, industrious citizens, and staunch, dependable breadwinners.   It was easy to understand why, after my father died in 1985, my brother, without saying so, became the default father in my life. Eight years his junior, I enjoyed having this renewed contact with him and soon realized that any sustainable relationship would be on his terms. Too many brothers' late-in-life friendships suffer due to a peculiar but biblical older-younger brother syndrome (e.g., Cane and Able, Esau and Jacob) in which I had no interest in partaking. For me, I would go along to get along.

Yet, a long-term issue within our relationship rose to test its mettle. As joint owner of our Skaneateles Lake property in Upstate New York since our mother passed, I had been trying to convince my elder sibling to deed a slice of its bare land to enable Emily and me to build a cottage. His undaunted adversity to "change" repeatedly overwhelmed his willingness to give way to my wishes. Wrestled I did with that will of his for over six years before until, bless his quintuple coronary bypassed heart, he relented. This was the first and only time I ever prevailed in a contest of wills with him. It taught me he could be convinced (or worn down) to give way in my favor. It also made me appreciate him as a just man and took it as a (long overdue) sign of respect. His reluctance to "change" issue remained unalterable enough for me to conclude that our real estate agreement would stand as the first and only memorial to my bulldog tenacity in our fraternal history. Wrong again.

Brotherly Ministry

Pulling the hospital room's only chair alongside his bed through its maze of tubes and wires, I settled in for the evening ahead. Our brotherly sojourn began by reminiscing about our earliest days when he would torment me mercilessly with "Dutch Rubs" (older bare knuckles scrubbing the top of a younger immobilized head), abandon me at every opportunity, and give me things like baby rattles for my eighth Christmas. (Fortunately, I had sleuthed out the "rattle plan," so I had ample time to prepare him a cheerily wrapped box of coal well in advance.) It was also a suitable time to chide him for repeated inquisitions where he pinned me to the ground on my back while straddling my chest, knees immobilizing my arms and threatening to launch bubbling saliva bombs into my mouth if I dared open it. This conversation was brilliantly timed and exquisitely conducted. He could not defend himself (any more than I could as a child, I might add), so we gratefully avoided sticky rebuttals or long-winded explanations devoid of apologies or facts. I chose our remaining one-sided dialogue that night to revolve around summer adventures at our Skaneateles Lake cottage. Not-so-bold to remind him I had the same emotional long-term investment as him in our shared heirloom, why would I risk what was already mine? In his heart, I knew with no doubt he considered that property his domain and me an interloper. Though lawfully without legs, it was one place I chose to never go to preserve my identity as a by-default brotherly peacekeeper. Why? Because he was worth it.

Satisfied that night with overcoming sixty-four years of self-enforced silence in one brief hour by courageously holding ground as a reasoning adult, I was equally pleased with his willingness, patience, and self-control, which had encouraged me to seek closure to all our under-addressed childhood brother issues. The change in him was simply exhilarating; that night he had given me a voice, even respect, by allowing his brother unchallenged freedom to speak without a single interruption. As a precaution, however, I sealed our evening by reading him selected biblical scriptures aloud, letting the words of Apostle Paul, whom he loved and quoted often, remind him of his Christian duty to appreciate his younger brother's loyalty and amputate any dangling participles in our rekindled relationship. Deep in my little conniving heart, however, I knew the entire evening I was living a pipedream, for he had not heard a single word during my entire soliloquy. That reality came with its own mountain of considerable relief. Finally, basking in my secure position let me throw caution to the wind and sing older Maranatha praise songs over him. Had he been responsive, we might have ended our late-night fellowship on those discordant notes, likely erasing what progress we made during the entire evening of our fraternal bonding. Let's hope that both older and younger brothers reading this story understand why I needed to use tongue-in-cheek to ramble through the past few paragraphs. Thank you for giving your precious time to help me struggle through this memorial to the brother I loved and now miss more than I could have ever imagined.

In a Valley of Decision

After our brotherly tête-à-tête, I checked to see that all his tubes were patent, the IV running, the catheter working, and his airway suctioned clear. Then, with the extra pillow and blanket, I curled up in my chair like a 200-pound Chihuahua, closed my eyes and dozed off. At 1:00 a.m., my brother's breathing was becoming erratic: rapid, deep breaths gradually gave way to ones slower and progressively shallower, only to rise in rate and depth again. This cyclical pattern (Cheyne-Stokes respirations) eventually did not reinitiate his breathing after one extended pause. Standing at his bedside and looking down at him reminded me of my father's passing years earlier. How similar in appearance had they become in their later years?

In addition to his respiratory failure, he soon lost all palpable pulses as his heart failed, and his skin turned that pale cyanotic blue that goes with passing. Had I been his personal doctor, with those fixed pupils, I would have pronounced him deceased. Yet, I was conflicted. As a clinician and a brother, I felt relief, for he was free after an exceedingly difficult five weeks and could now rest in the Lord. Simultaneously, I wrestled with two thoughts: The first took me to the verses in Philippians (1:23–24), where Paul prefers to be with Christ while knowing it would be better that he remained with those on earth who needed him. The second was my sister-in-law's deep wish to be with her husband when he passed. For days, she had camped at his bedside to avoid missing this unfolding event. What personal anguish for her not to be here!

"Lord Jesus, I don't know what to do," I confessed in quiet desperation. Instantly, a familiar inner witness, a clear and overwhelming unction, convinced me it was not his time. Holy Spirit had spoken, in violation of my brother's durable power of attorney and my good sense as a clinician, I must add. Well, what to do? Unresponsive for weeks, lifeless for minutes, and contrary to any physician's good sense but obedient to the Spirit, I bent over and placed my hands on his chest to start simple chest compressions. After the first few, I paused. No vital signs. Then, more compressions. Still, nothing. The third time, a small breath. I successfully repeated this formula but soon concluded these were futile attempts to revive him. Mouth-to-mouth resuscitation or calling for a crash cart or a ventilator were not options. Gazing down, for some unknown reason, I spoke to this clinically dead man,

"Brother, you can't leave your wife like Mom left Dad. You knew how devastated our father was to miss her passing by mere moments. Please make certain that your wife makes it to yours."

Throughout this intense appeal, my brother was lying lifeless and ashen, no more than the corpse he had become. Then, for another unknown reason, maybe out of frustration or even faith, in my finest Marine command voice, I boomed, "I want you to breathe—now!" (It seems peculiar, does it not, that his long-term, unresponsive, comatose state and recent loss of life never influenced my thoughts or actions? But not peculiar to Jesus.) When he answered with a breath, I nearly lost mine. Astonished, I stammered, "Good. Now, take another!" So, he did. Then, for the next hours, Jesus, my brother, and I, using those chest compressions, words of encouragement, and renewed purpose, worked toward two ends: unassisted breathing now and his wife's arrival in the morning.

All Things Work Together

By 5:00 a.m., his breathing was spontaneous, regular, and strong, and his color back to normal. It was as if he had never passed. Sitting down, I took his hand and, between periods of my own broken sleep, continued to encourage him. His wife, I shared, would arrive in three hours. Parenthetically, to this point, he had shown no response beyond a pulse and willingness to breathe. At 8:00 a.m., one of his sons called to ask of his condition, while at 9:00 a.m., my sister-in-law let me know she and my wife were on their way. At 9:30 a.m., my brother began wrestling with his breathing again. At 9:45 a.m., I stood watching him struggle more and ventilate less. At 10:00 a.m., straight up, I poised, ready to lend a hand by reinstating chest compressions while encouraging him on with, "Brother, keep it up. Just a couple minutes, and she will be here." In cadence with those words, his wife, Karen, entered the room, went directly to his bedside, leaned close, kissed his cheek, and cheerfully followed with, "Good morning, Hugh, I love you."

Whoa! Then it happened, something that I had not seen in over thirty years of medicine: my comatose brother, his body paralyzed for weeks, unresponsive to all stimuli, diagnosed terminal and brain-dead by a local neurologist, opened his eyes, focused them upon his wife, rose six inches off the pillow, twice mouthed the words, "I love you," gave a thumbs up to my Emily, and then, smiling ear to ear, collapsed breathless, pulseless, lifeless, and grayer than a New York winter upon his pillow.

Postscript

Later, as I worked through that astonishing night, it was clear my brother died at 3:00 a.m. Then the Lord, privileging me as His assistant, revived and placed him on "life support" until my sister-in-law arrived at ten o'clock the following morning. How do I conclude this? After dying in my presence, should he have breathed on command? No. Even if we believed he had not died but continued unresponsive in a comatose state as he had for weeks? No. When his wife arrived, should he, for five weeks paralyzed, comatose, and diagnosed brain-dead, opened his eyes, risen conscious from his pillow in an unscheduled Lazarus moment (a brief period of awareness occasionally known to humans before death), mouthed his last words, smiled, given Emily a thumbs up, and collapsed? No.

Commonly, a person closing in on death slows breathing gradually (as my brother had earlier), not instantaneously. When respirations weaken and finally stop, the heart also steadily slows and deteriorates into an arrhythmia before flatlining, as appeared the case at 3:00 a.m. That morning at 10:00 a.m., however, his vital signs came to a dead stop (forgive the play on words). Why did both his breathing and heart stop instantly and at the same moment? Again, I suggest my brother died at 3:00 a.m. when Holy Spirit intervened to place him on seven hours of "life support" to assure final goodbyes with his wife. Right after that, he resumed his postmortem 3:00 a.m. state and journey to Jesus.

Is there a single doubt that my brother saved his wife, Karen, from potential years of grief (maybe guilt, shame, and disappointment) by his love and willingness to partner with a compassionate Jesus to extract one final unselfish moment from his life to bless hers? It was so like him to be considerate to the end. Then, as the pièce de résistance, in His eagerness to not only choreograph the event, the Lord punctuated it with the finest of final Kisses from Heaven, an unscheduled Lazarus moment and as gracious and purposeful a last moment Karen could have wished for—and all the sweeter because she did.

Isn't the Lord good!

QUESTION: Where is the Kiss from Heaven in this God Story?

ANSWER: Well, we covered this adequately, but to put a little icing on that cake, let's summarize: My brother, in a coma and pronounced "brain-dead" by a neurologist for five solid weeks, clinically died on my watch at 3:00 a.m., was resurrected by the Lord with a little help from his brother, and placed on life support by Heaven for five hours until his wife arrived to say goodbye. At that precise time, he gained consciousness, in a Lazarus moment, rose in the bed to bid his goodbyes, and then, without vital signs, completed his interrupted journey to Jesus begun at 3:00 a.m. in a nanosecond.

Wow, what an extraordinary Kiss from Heaven for my sister-in-law, the rest of us at his bedside, and three hundred people responding with amazement as this God Story was shared at his service. And wasn't it all carried out decently and in order (1 Cor.14:40). Wasn't that what my brother would have considered essential had he known what was on the way? To tell the truth, had the man his say, that tale would never have made it out of committee. What a miracle and Kiss from Heaven . . . I had my way again.

Goodbye, Grandpa (2003)

Well, it was finished; we had laid my brother to rest on a hillside nearby the shores of Skaneateles Lake, the clearest and most coveted of all Central New York State's magnificent Finger Lakes. It nearly took a court order to supersede the cemetery procedure to bury his casket facing east toward that well-known body of water he dearly loved his entire life. Another reason for that decision? Maybe to be the first on that hillside to herald the moment of Jesus' return to the rest of his manicured row, all facing west. Who knew? What we did know was this man's last wish, after a lifetime steeped in tradition, unwavering cooperation, and adherence to the rule of law, was one of glaring nonconformity. If you ever need proof that the odds eventually do catch up, look no further. Overcoming his breach of burial protocol and to his credit, my brother had gone beyond expectations by detailing his entire funeral service with the skill of a Swiss watchmaker.

Following the service, the family gathered at his graveside, extended final adieus, and then moved to my sister-in-law's home in Rochester to share a meal. At the completion of that elegant culinary event, I excused myself and retired to my brother's office, its walls lined with generations of family photographs, multiple awards, and personal treasures, including a generous scattering of our late father's hand-me-downs.

Ceiling lights dimmed to creamy velvet cast willowy shadows over the room's cluttered walls, making it hard to place each piece of memorabilia in proper sequence to sort through his life. Unexpectantly interrupting my quest, the silhouette of a little girl leaning against the door frame entering the adjacent lighted living room caught my attention. For a brief time, she stood motionless and silent until, with genuine sadness, I heard her whisper, "Grandpa, are you going away and not coming back?"

At that moment, I recognized the little silhouette's voice belonged to Katie, one of my brother's sweet granddaughters, mistaking me for her grandfather. Oh my, I had no idea how to respond. While my mind was futilely seeking words sensitive enough to correct her impression, the Lord gently held my tongue. Looking back, might this have been a divine appointment and a time of closure for Katie? If so, how so? Well, try this for size: Suddenly, without warning and seemingly out of nowhere, here came Someone using my voice without asking permission: "Yes, Katie," spoke the voice full of kindness and understanding, "Grandpa is going away but will see you again. Always remember Grandpa loves you."

Katie, receiving her Kiss from Heaven (and me mine), said no more. Her silhouette faded seconds later, slipping back into a distant kitchen to play happily with her cousins. From outward appearances, it seemed that recent dialogue resulted in little more than a fortuitous outcome for an irreconcilable conundrum. Au contraire, my Christian friend, it meant so much more. To see our wise and sometimes wily Holy Spirit enter incognito at the eleventh hour to bring little Katie the answer she desperately needed and mercifully pluck heavenly tongue-tied me from that sticky conundrum was beyond compare. For those Kisses from Heaven alone, we must be grateful. That afternoon, I was grateful, so grateful to the One who never leaves or forsakes us, the One who is our everlasting help in times of trouble. I'd wager Katie was grateful too. After all, she would see her Grandpa again.

Postscript

Katie never again mistook me for my brother, although I must confess, she erred by calling me Grandpa occasionally for a year or two. How that warmed my heart! What was that all about, anyway? Was it as simple as Holy Spirit needing a replacement grandpa from the same side of the family to love her for a while? My brother would have liked that. Or did the Spirit believe I needed another granddaughter to love? That thought blessed me. Could it have been that simple? Sometimes, I wonder if we should license the position of grandpa like a pastor, doctor, or social worker rather than one classified as an elderly relative two generations removed with whom you are expected to occasionally exchange visits. That could supply a grandpa's love to more children who have never known but genuinely need that special brand of affection. Think what would happen if all the out-of-work grandpas could move into the workplace. Wouldn't that be a shot in the arm for the economy? Talk about creating jobs! And what a blessing for so many discarded, used-up old guys and broken little kids who do not even know they need each other.

More than likely, it would "deeply concern" the more politically correct crowds when the grandpas did not fit the right bloodline, skin color, religious persuasion, rung on the economic ladder, educational degree, or social position. But what is new? I wonder if those discriminating and "deeply concerned" folks—who might think or feel that unconditional love needs to be restricted, defined, or at least managed by well-thought-out objectives, emotionally detached lists of rules and requirements, doctrines and dogmas, bloodlines, ideologies, philosophies, or statutes and court decisions—should also include input from all those neglected, abused, and brokenhearted little kids missing grandpas and starving for their love?

I do not have all the answers to those questions, but knowing how Jesus feels about little ones, you can bet your bottom dollar, even to the last penny, that He would be more than willing to share His lap with every child needing one.

"But Jesus said, 'Let the little children alone, and do not hinder them from coming to Me; for the kingdom of Heaven belongs to such as these'" (Matt. 19:14). Wow, did you ever consider your lap to be as the kingdom of Heaven on Earth for your grandbabies, Grandpa? What a blessed thought and privilege . . . but, oh my, the grief when denied.

QUESTION: What is the Kiss from Heaven in this God Story?

ANSWER: Katie was grieving. Her Grandpa died, and she had been told he was going away. Worse, she thought I was he. Then Katie asked if she would see him again. Oh, I was stuck with what to say or if I should say anything at all. Then, I was immediately reminded of Psalm 81:10, and if I opened my mouth, He would fill it. (I wish Luke 12:12 had come to mind that the Holy Spirit will give us the words to say at the moment we need them. But no such comfort came.) So, there I was waiting with my mouth gaping, wordless, and mimicking a wide-open crevasse, when by faith and patience (Heb. 6:12), those promises came forth with no effort on my part: "Yes, Katie, Grandpa is going away but will see you again. Always remember that Grandpa loves you." Then, fully satisfied it seemed, Katie slid back into her now-untroubled little girl life while my crevasse and I moved on to thank our Savior for once more doing what He promised: saving me . . . again.

Little Shelby Jones (2004)

We have noticed over the years that while western North America's "snowbirds" gravitate to Arizona for the winter, the eastern folks migrate to Florida. It only makes sense, given the travel needed. After that fashion, the heartlands of the United States and Canada tend toward South Texas and a place curiously called the Rio Grande Valley.

Now a valley, to those having lived in higher latitudes, conjures up mental images of lush green fields and pastures bordering meandering crystal streams or rivers sandwiched between towering snow-capped mountains or, at the very least, readily definable hillsides. Well, let me suggest that you not be in a hurry to bring your climbing gear or white-water kayaks to the Rio Grande Valley for a South Texas winter. Look, what Texans call a "valley" looks more like the Lord took a wrong turn ferrying His steamroller to Kansas. This "valley," to a Northerner, is "flatter than a pancake" and the mighty Rio Grande River, as it empties into the Gulf of Mexico that time of the year, more like the stream from an eighty-five-year-old grandpa. (As a doctor, I reserve the right to use medical analogies.)

Anyway, just do not forget to bring a big ole sombrero, multiple canteens, sunblock, bug spray, snake bite kits, and a handheld GPS. South Texas, friend, is a big ole hot desert, a real armadillo, roadrunner, rattlesnake infested, and cactus kind of desert! Ain't no respectable valley I ever seen in these parts, that's fer sure. And I been here bout long nuf to be talkin' like these folks . . . pardner.

A Tenderhearted Tragedy

While in Texas, we went to a friendly, rapidly growing little church in Laguna Vista, a slower-growing community a handful of miles to the northeast of Port Isabel and the Queen Isabella Causeway to South Padre Island, a shining sand spit running north all the way to Galveston which, itself, is far enough away to be a foreign country. Do I have you oriented?

A young forward-thinking pastor, Ernest Jones, started the fellowship, which flourished quickly, added a new sanctuary, and grew over a four-year period to over three hundred locals and winter Texans, the Lone Star State's handle for "snowbirds."

Identified as a winter Texan connects you to the general population in an inclusive way, the way most Texans welcome visitors. That hospitality spilled over into Christ Harbor Church, an independent Southern Baptist fellowship (figure that one out if you can), where something was always happening, people were encouraged to exercise their gifts, and the preacher never delivered a sub-par sermon. Emily and I were soon at work presenting Ed Glaspey's Restoration Video Series (Junction City, Oregon) two nights a week to lay the foundation for individual inner healing sessions down the line.

The pastor and his wife were Nathan's and Shelby's parents. Now, Nathan was a stout six while Shelby was a tousled towhead of three when it happened. Sounds scary right off the bat, doesn't it? Well, friend, it was.

Late one blazing hot Saturday morning, while Pastor was busily rustling up Sunday's sermon in the cool of the church office, his well-intentioned young son was considerately carrying his barefoot little sister above the red-hot pavers leading to the church's entrance.

Well, misfortune struck when Nathan dropped Shelby; to make matters worse, he dropped her squarely on her ringlets! Shelby cried before her mom came to the rescue and took her home while urging her concerned husband to let me know. Like a good dad, Pastor Jones did. However, information from the "horse's mouth" is always preferable to getting it secondhand, so I called Shelby's mom. Apparently, Nathan shared his sister had not lost consciousness but cried right after striking her head, was now resting, had a headache, and wished to sleep (the behavior of choice for most traumatized kids). Now, doctors know that head injuries in kids are always a risky business and often unappreciated for the "time bombs" they potentially are. So, I talked to her mom about the symptoms and signs on which she should keep her eye, including changes in her level of consciousness, seizures, persistent sleepiness after a nap, difficulty rousing Shelby from sleep, confusion, nausea, vomiting, persistent headache and so forth. She checked the equality and size of her daughter's pupils for me, which seemed normal and equal. As I recall, she summarized that, though sleepy, her little girl was walking, talking, and being a tad sassy as usual.

Insisting she rush Shelby to the hospital, a full thirty minutes away as the Egret flies, were she to manifest any warning signals, I set about preparing to visit the little munchkin within the hour. It was not minutes before my phone rang. Shelby had vomited, and her dependable mom was already sprinting her way to the hospital in Harlingen.

Domino-Like Events

This is not an in-depth factual report of the entire medical history surrounding that day but more a brief but comprehensive overview, a human-interest story at its core. As you read this vignette, composed directly after the fact (edited later), know that trauma causes more fatalities in the United States than any other condition or disease in Shelby's age group. Here, in this little girl's case, we should take note that 50 percent of these trauma deaths occur from head injuries.

Where was God when you were injured, Shelby Jones? In the heart of your daddy, who chose to "disturb" the doctor on a Saturday? In the heart of your mommy, who promptly followed instructions to bring you to the hospital after you vomited? In the heart of the intercessors, who prayed as you were racing toward medical help? In the hearts of the weekend emergency room staff, who admitted you at once and scheduled your CT scan within minutes of arrival on a weekend evening when you might have waited hours? In the hearts of a praying church as the word spread quickly through the congregation? In the heart of a neurosurgeon, who responded with dispatch and compassion when called from a family gathering? In the hearts of an operating room team, who rapidly assembled to help that doctor save the life of a little three-year-old? In the hearts of your mommy and daddy's friends and family, who called and came to pray and give comfort? In the heart of an island (South Padre Island) pastor, who came to support his brother of the cloth? In the heart of a neighborhood doctor who called his neurosurgeon friend in the operating suite midway through the surgery to seek assurance for the family that all things were going well? In the hearts of the pediatric ICU staff, who counseled and comforted your parents and you during your brief tenure in that scary place? Yes, Shelby, in the hearts of every soul pouring his or her gifts into the threatened life of a single desperate little girl suffering from a treacherous injury.

Where was God, little Shelby Jones, during your injury? Where He always is, in the hearts of His people, extending mercy and comfort into the lives of His distressed ones, listening to the prayers of an interceding church, and then directing and guiding those who will hear His voice to minister His love and healing to those in need.

On Tuesday, Shelby will be home and seem little different (well, minus those ringlets) for her ordeal. Most (but not all) of us will soon forget this tumultuous weekend carved out of the busyness of our lives. An expedited visit of a desperately ill little child into and out of the quagmire of weekend city hospital medicine will be assumed the "norm," what should always happen, and what any of us should expect in these days of advanced technology.

Then, sadly, there are those among us who will let the hidden hand of God slip away, unappreciated after working His miracle. Then, others who marveled at His handiwork will return to their daily routines, tempted to assign the managing of this weekend's perilous event to good timing, good fortune, sound medical professionalism, and a little luck. Such are the ways of rational men.

Jesus, forgive us for the veils draped over our eyes, the dullness of our hearing, the deception in our minds, and the hardness in our hearts that so often prevent us from seeing your ever-present hand at work. Thank you for reminding us of your faithfulness in last weekend's blessed outcome, Lord. Thank you for your mercy. Thank you for your grace. Thank you for preserving little Shelby's life, for being her Savior, and once more proving who you are to all of us. We give you all the glory.

Twenty Minutes

Shelby sustained a fracture to her skull in that inadvertent fall. The fracture line ran through a groove in the bone on the inside of her temple. In that groove traveled the middle meningeal artery, a major vessel now cruelly torn and pumping blood into the spaces surrounding Shelby's little brain. The danger, as the pressure increased steadily inside her skull due to an accumulation of blood, lay in the real possibility that part of her brain might herniate to cause a rapid death. The neurosurgeon said as he completed her surgery that Shelby had but twenty minutes left before he intervened to avoid that tragedy.

Twenty minutes? That's not enough time to take Saturday night's bath, young lady. That's not time enough to fix your hair, girl. That's not time enough to walk to church to see Daddy. Or hear a bedtime story. Or open your birthday presents. Or watch your favorite TV show! But it was time enough, was it not, for Jesus, the grand organizer of each of our personal universes and well-skilled at getting things done perfectly and in time, to give our baby girl a second chance. There were a whole lot of links in the chain that the Lord had to join in a big hurry to ensure the successful outcome of Shelby's nip-and-tuck drama. Had but one taken added seconds, the outcome may have ended in sorrow. But for Shelby's Kiss from Heaven.

Postscript

Honestly, it was hard for everyone to see this petite towhead sweetie pie pressing against death's door without a good reason as if being dropped squarely on her noggin had not been reason enough. After surgery, Shelby seemed a tad contemplative if that is possible for a three-year-old. She was calmer, happier, and smiled much more easily than she had before her accident while acting a tad like someone who might have had a near-death experience and seen Jesus.

I never asked about that possibility, and, over time, Shelby did what we so often do as humans: She slipped back into business as usual. It was heartwarming to see this little girl not negatively changed by her trauma in a physical sense, but it caused me no small amount of sadness to see the glory of His presence fade over time from that little girl's face after her special Kiss from Heaven. Still, as a confidence, I cling to this hope, more an assurance learned years ago: No one touched by the Master will ever be satisfied with the "ordinary" or ever be the same again. So, I am prone to confidently subscribe to the wisdom of the prophet Yogi (Berra), who once said, "It's not over (little Shelby Jones) until it's over."

And don't you know, it wasn't over, and wouldn't you love to hear the rest of this story? But then it's about the same God, so no surprise ... well, not to Nurse Shelby anyway.

QUESTION: Where is the Kiss from Heaven in this God Story?

ANSWER: Shelby to Nathan to Pastor to Mom to Pastor to me to Mom to a hospital to an ER registration to an ER triage nurse exam to an ER nurse exam to an ER doctor exam to a CT scan to a radiologist reading to an ER doctor to a neurosurgeon's consult to a surgery suite prep to Shelby's prep to her surgery procedure. There were over twenty human interactions, communications, trips, exams, decisions, preps, and procedures before that torn and gushing middle meningeal artery (forming an epidural hematoma leading to the risk of brain herniation and death) was corralled and brought under control. The neurosurgeon said Shelby had but twenty minutes to live had it not been for the prompt surgical intervention.

Consider this: Had each of those twenty interactions taken sixty seconds or longer, Shelby would have been on her way to Heaven. A slight delay here or there. A stoplight. A need for gas or a potty break. Another preemptive emergency. The scanner in use. The operating suite occupied. And on and on.

Take heart, Christian. No problem for a God who orders the steps of two billion five hundred million believers, keeps track of two hundred billion trillion stars, and names five hundred million new ones every day. Think of what Jesus can do with twenty minutes. What was the hurry? Why, He had time to hang and name another seven million baby stars before taking care of our one baby girl. But considerate as Jesus is, He focused on Shelby and all those interceding family and folks pleading for her life to show up twenty minutes early.

Come on, friend, we all know it takes our God no time at all to perform a miracle.

A Full Meal Deal (2010)

A venerable side trip for all tourists trekking Uganda is one to the equator, an invisible line in the sand we were straddling, one foot in either hemisphere, while on a mission trip to Show Mercy International's growing community, the Field of Dreams, fourteen miles as the crow flies from the capital city of Kampala. Memorable about that side trip were three outside comfort stations without privacy walls, clearly visible in the wide-open spaces but the three most popular privies in the entire vicinity. That is correct. Surrounded by gift shops and well-guarded by what appeared from a distance to be a full-time security agent, those three open-air toilets, lined up three to four people deep, were without question the busiest. How could that be? They were all in plain sight. Had these Ugandan people no modesty? No decorum? No regard for the more delicate sensibilities of the Western tourist? Have you ever jumped to a conclusion when you do not have all the information? I had.

Privy Science

Here are facts of which you may not be aware. Water flushed down a commode placed directly over the equator plunges in a straight line down the privy's drain. (Remember, geometry students, a straight line is the shortest distance between two points.) Otherwise, the water takes its sweet time swirling its way counterclockwise down an identical toilet found a couple of feet south of the equator in the Southern Hemisphere but clockwise a couple of feet to the north in the Northern Hemisphere. It took minutes (and dollars) to wait in a short line (which got to feel longer while "broasting" in an unrelenting equatorial sun) to see that less-than-jaw-dropping three-privy-physics-project-phenomena presented as that day's lesson in physical science. Voilà, three popular commodes, three successful experiments, and on to the bank for one entrepreneurial Ugandan business owner, until now presumed a security guard.

Freshly educated, others of our team then visited the indoor and more tourist-sensitive water closets (which, for no money at all, illustrated with precision, and in the privacy of cool shelters, selected parts of their more costly outdoor cousins' principles of physics) before boarding the bus where I had inadvertently left my wallet unattended.

An Aside

Wallet returned the following day, credit card numbers having unwittingly found their way into the hands of another local entrepreneur who would spend many carefree hours flying first class about Africa over the next six months before my Yankee-bulldog-can-do-tenacity sleuthed that thief out with the help of Visa investigators in Belgium (who I need to thank again) all the way to his apprehension by airport authorities on one delightful (for me at least) morning while boarding yet another flight I had subsidized in nearby Kenya to end this whodunnit. Apologies for that extraordinarily long run-on sentence, but it had been an extraordinarily long teachable day, regrettably turned extraordinarily longer teachable six months while costing extraordinarily more tuition for the lesson learned than I could ever have predicted. While it did take a chunk of time to navigate our way through that Uganda credit card drama, I assure you we took no time at all to enroll in Life Lock.

Our Déjà Vu Jesus

Saturday morning's lunch for fifty children in the little Muslim village, a stone's throw up the road from the Field of Dreams, was a true Christian witness to a pure Muslim population. Within an hour, that effort blossomed to two hundred kids after word of the free meal spread throughout the district. Early that morning, volunteers had begun busily cooking enormous pots of rice, beans, potatoes, and (as I may incorrectly recall) mystery meat over roaring outside fires. The excitement among those adult Christian workers and the children in attendance was palpable as rising decibels of joyous fellowship filled the air until one savvy soul counted the extra one hundred fifty children that the celebration was ill-equipped to feed.

Among those readying the meal, the mood pivoted suddenly to melancholy and then to decibels of despair. Women openly wept and soon pled together in prayer for Jesus to do as He had done before: "Please, Lord, multiply our scant supply." With intercessors in action, the remaining volunteers continued to serve bold portions of food in faith to each child, ranging from toddlers to teens seated at dozens of large rough-hewn tables crammed into a barn-sized room. Sitting among them while holding an eighteen-month-old toddler on my lap, being hand-fed by his sister from the plate we held in common, I palpated the little guy's enlarged spleen plunging toward his pelvic bowl. He, like so many children, one in five born in Sub-Sahara Africa, unlikely to see a fifth birthday due to tropical disease or the AIDS virus, was odds on already the victim of the dreaded malaria parasite. Later that day, I came upon two five-year-old boys, each in a coma with a high fever, lying on the dirt floor among their busy friends. It was the way of rural Uganda, where medical care for significant disease was (at the time) only possible by traveling to larger urban hospitals.

Those two little munchkins would probably die. The sweet little one in my lap would be a strong candidate to follow. It caused me no little distress.

My troubled thoughts, rudely interrupted by women shouting and hollering again from the kitchen, prompted me to deliver baby to his little sister and rush toward the bedlam. On the way, jubilant workers hurried by loaded down with overflowing plates, tears streaming down their faces, and voices praising Jesus for answered prayer. Why? Well, the Lord was multiplying what food remained. Emily was already rejoicing with the rest of the folks gathered around the pots when I arrived.

Sure enough, kettles were staying level with food despite continuous generous portions being scooped from their unchanging depths. As the news spread, even enterprising adults appeared in the lengthening line seeking free food. No problem. On and on came the servings until the volunteer workers were blessed to send innumerable takeout dinners home with the children as the event ended. (If you wish more, Google the YouTube entry for January 25, 2010, "Food Multiplication in Uganda," for an in-depth report and to see yours truly, and a generous forty more pounds of him, sharing a meal with the little guy and his sister.)

Postscript

Food multiplication is not a unique event in the annals of Christian gatherings, but it was a well-timed welcomed Kiss from Heaven on that glorious Saturday morning. Missionary evangelists say as armies march on their stomachs so does a world steeped in poverty. Over the years, free food sources by themselves have enticed countless underfed unbelievers to temporarily remodel their belief systems to follow Jesus for culinary reasons alone, only to leave Him when the tables are cleared. These temporary additions to the Church are dubbed "Milk Christians." We can safely assume that the Lord, to glue such folks more permanently to Himself, has used added ways from the Sermon on the Mount to dramatic attesting miracles (healing diseases and delivering demons) to prove Himself (Matt.11:2), build greater faith in others, and give folks reasons to follow Him well beyond filling an empty belly. Sometimes, that has worked, and sadly, sometimes it has not.

Jesus ran into the latter predicament after He fed the five thousand (John 6:10–13), followed by conquering a major storm while walking the Sea of Galilee. By the following day, the account of His food multiplication, having spread to surrounding towns, prompted boatloads to pursue Him across the water from distant Tiberias. The Lord greeted them and cut to the chase: "Truly, truly, I say to you, you seek Me, not because of the signs, but because you ate of the loaves and were filled" (John 6:26). Those who had seen or heard of the previous day's miracle demanded a fresh sign (expecting another free meal, we presume) and illustrating their focus went no further than their bellies.

For these opportunists, the miracles were merely means to an end and of far more interest than the miracle worker Himself. When Jesus did not accommodate the Galileans' demands but instead offered spiritual food by preaching a bottom-line biblical word, the interlopers took offense and left (John 6:66). (Whoa, check that address.) How often do we see folks driven by what miracles do for their flesh instead of building their spirits and drawing them closer to Jesus? Too often! Of the ten healed lepers, what number returned to thank Jesus and glorify God (Luke 17:18)? A tithe's worth. Ten percent. One Samaritan. Sadly, add me to that list more than once.

When you have been a Christian for decades, it is clear, as it was to the Apostle Paul early in his ministry, that what organized Christianity often offers is but metaphorical fish and bread for the flesh (today by way of Christian television, movies, concerts, clubs, schools, summer camps, weekend "revivals," etc.) while failing to train converts to fish for a lifetime as disciples in the Spirit. When we ignore instilling true elemental principles (Heb. 6), essential biblical Christian doctrine gluing newborns to the faith, we risk leaving Jesus with abandoned baby Christians, non-discipled converts who never move past the short-term fish (i.e., the joy of salvation, honeymoon periods wasted when hunger for discipleship is at its peak, and, eventually, discouraged backsliding Christians futilely groping their way toward, but rarely reaching maturity). These are those who become our neglected modern-day "Milk Christians."

Here appears a paradox not actually a paradox. You ask, "Didn't Apostle Paul state that we must lay aside the elemental principles of the faith and press on to maturity?" (Heb. 6:1–2). Absolutely! But first, and essential to our understanding, Paul was speaking to disciples already conditioned by reflex to use those elemental principles (doctrine) as a foundation to press into the things of the Spirit. Second, what Paul meant by movement to maturity was "that you are not sluggish, but imitators of those who through faith and patience inherit the promises" (Heb. 6:12).

In this discussion, once elemental principles (fundamental doctrine) are ingrained in new Christians, those disciples must press onward in the Spirit by faith (assurance of God's unseen promises) and patience (forbearance until they are fulfilled). This means no longer being bound to human will to enforce those elemental principles by rote but dependent upon Holy Spirit's wisdom and power to walk faithfully and patiently into what God has promised as our inheritance to please the Father and bring Him glory.

A Reminder

If you are hungry for your own Kiss from Heaven, then schedule a mission trip to the Field of Dreams to see for yourself an example of bedrock Christianity manifested by Holy Spirit using praying believers to carry out miracles. What do I mean? Well, weren't you, by proxy at least, a recent witness to intercessors who went beyond the limits of human will by faith and patience in the Spirit to move Jesus to miraculously feed an extra one hundred fifty Ugandan children and participating adults by multiplying everything edible in sight on a bright Saturday morning during a little Muslim village's impromptu breakfast miracle?

That journey to the Field of Dreams will be worth your while. While there, do not forget to take in that renowned equatorial privy science. Remember to use an inside comfort station to save a couple of greenbacks and avoid a "broasting."

Oh, one more thing, Christian—keep an eye on your wallet.

QUESTION: Where is the Kiss from Heaven in this God Story?

ANSWER: Wish you could have been there. A room packed full of little kids eating voraciously at tables on benches, the dirt floor, and, don't forget, the little guy sitting on my lap. Then came the shouting and hollering led by Lori Salley, co-founder of Show Mercy International Ministries, running up and down the aisle, announcing the food was multiplying. Then those serving, who had been weeping for the lack of food needed (due to an unexpected onslaught of little kids and adults from everywhere), suddenly were shedding tears of joy because the Lord was supplying an overabundance of everything. Yes, Emily checked it out. Me too. No doubt, the ladles were working overtime to keep up with distributing the increased supply. Whoa, wasn't this a modern-day microcosm of when Jesus fed the five thousand—but with added takeout, no leftovers, and no need to clean up afterward. What a gigantic Kiss from Heaven and testimony to the goodness of God in the land of the living (Ps. 27:13).

True Compassion (2010)

Let us cut to the chase: For the last few years, since my heart attacks and stentings, I had taken a fistful of medications to keep the old ticker ticking. Included was a beta blocker, a class of pharmaceuticals found effective in reducing the work of the heart, the risk of angina (heart pain due to oxygen lack), and the risk of repeated infarction (heart muscle injury and death). Mental health professionals also use these drugs to moderate their patients' moods; a beta blocker blunts feelings and flattens emotions. So, for over three years, to realize the beneficial effects of this beta blocker, it had been necessary to accept a certain curtailment of my emotional life. That translated to a degree of mental numbness, reduced feelings of compassion, and a limited ability to weep. Now, do not assume these medications erase one's emotional life or create a zombie-like state. By no means. However, they may create an impasse when getting in touch with one's own feelings, but, more devastating, cause a Christian to struggle feeling God's presence.

Emily and I had recently returned from Uganda after visiting a vast number of children orphaned by war (the Sudanese civil war to the north), poverty, malaria, AIDS, and other tropical maladies. Truthfully, for yours truly, the trip had been somewhat of a paradox. Most missionary journeys over the previous thirty years had been effusions of joy, mercy, and compassion for the less fortunate and punctuated by hesitation to leave those people behind when time to return stateside. This adventure had been different. Oh, our resolute team members were wonderful companions; everyone bonded and interacted with ease while visiting hospitals, orphanages, and schools while ministering to the medical, emotional, and spiritual needs of both our team members and the Ugandan kids. The struggle arose when those daily journeys and times of ministry left me emotionally flat to the extent I nearly looked forward to going home. For what reason? That dratted beta blocker blunting my feelings. Not much of an other-centered experience, was it?

A Sunday Service Blindside

Well, here we were weeks following our return from Africa, ready to enjoy a glorious Sunday morning of praise and worship with our church family in Oregon. Regrettably, that morning turned out more glorious for some than others. To the degree I could not yet touch the hem of His garment nor quite enter His presence, I remained desperate and pleading, "I need more of you, Lord. Please help me get by this confounded beta blocker and experience you in worship again." Sadly, after the last three years, I had yet to accept this blunted emotional state as the way things were to be (i.e., my new normal).

Somewhere during my time of pleading with Jesus, I glimpsed our pastor, Denny Cline, standing in the aisle directly behind us. Within moments, he left only to return with an unfamiliar young woman but, as I later learned, not so to the local body for her sensitivity to the Spirit. Within minutes, she left, followed by Pastor returning to the front of the sanctuary.

Microphone in hand, he spoke, "I have been walking around this morning and came upon a place of interest. So, I asked Linda (not her given name) to come along to see if she sensed anything in the Spirit as we toured the aisles. She pointed out the identical area to which I had been drawn." Pastor then continued, "We have a couple who recently returned from Uganda."

A vocal friend thundered our names from the congregation without solicitation.

"Yes," seconded Pastor and, without skipping a beat, asked Emily and me to come up front. "All those in the congregation who would like an impartation (Rom. 1:11) of compassion, come forward, and this couple will lay hands upon you."

Taken by surprise, Emily and I, seeing no way to escape or evade, hesitantly left our seats and reluctantly inched forward at little more than a snail's pace. *What are you doing, Pastor?* I was thinking. *I haven't one thimble full of compassion available in my entire body. It's that beta blocker in the way again. No way can I do this; please, Lord, help Emily pick up the slack today.*

Entering the bright lights, one arm wrapped about the other's waist, we reached out with our remaining hands to touch the growing numbers of eager saints now lined up across the large sanctuary. At first contact, Emily and I broke into our spiritual languages, wept (more like sobbed) profusely in unison, and were soon "slinging snot," as the old Pentecostal Church had long ago dubbed that manifestation.

Meanwhile, those on the other side and targets of this ad hoc ministry were serially collapsing to the floor inebriated—but not as you suppose (Acts 2:15)—weeping as vociferously as we or wobbling in place like vertiginous Gumbys under Holy Spirit's grasp. Unable to fathom why we were weeping with so much intensity while feeling little near the level of emotion or glory going on about us was highly confusing. During the more intense moments, I felt like a detached observer of the whole out-of-control scene. After twenty minutes (it had become a longer line), Emily and I came to the line's end and, using an alternate route, returned to our seats by skirting the dogpile of humanity still "soaking" or recovering on the carpet at the front of the sanctuary.

Curiously, the first Christians upon whom we laid hands were two of the body's main intercessors, while the final two were saints who had known mental illness. Holy Spirit freely imparted His compassion to fill a whole spectrum of needs found in our church body that day. We had not spoken a handful of words in English the entire time; instead, both prayed without passion in the Spirit, which contradicted our snot-slinging and everyone else dropping as sacks of potatoes on the carpet.

When we do not know how to pray, and that day we did not, we are told to depend on Holy Spirit to intercede because He knows the will of God (Rom. 8:27). So, we had. Nearly dehydrated and spent from what had been an intense, although brief time, we wedged ourselves among the congregation again as if nothing had happened. Then, except for catching our breath, consuming copious amounts of *agua* from Emily's ever-present water bottle, and scrubbing defiant mascara streaks from her cheeks, we sat back to feed on Pastor's word for the day.

Trying to Figure It Out

What was that brief interlude all about? Looking back, wasn't there an open Heaven in that service where Holy Spirit changed my understanding of the roots and impartation of compassion? We all wish, even expect, an overflow of merciful feelings when ministering to hungry and needy folks. The compassion Jesus felt drove Him to perform miracles by feeding the hungry, healing the sick, or ministering to the downcast and depressed (Matt. 9:36). Compassion moves us in the same way. However, there were times, such as when the Lord called out the woman with the issue of blood, toyed with the

Syrophoenician mother for pestering Him, or rebuked His whining disciples after hushing the vicious storm on the Sea of Galilee for having little faith, when the Lord Himself seemed unready, interrupted, rushed, stressed, tired, or frustrated with someone in need and a candidate for a little compassion Himself. Still, He never failed to go to the folks who asked for help; however, it appeared that occasionally, He ministered with less than a full complement of compassion, even a little attitude.

In times past, Emily and I had relied on our levels of compassion as barometers to direct us when to minister. In our post-Uganda Sunday service, that reliance ended up like a beached whale when we laid hands upon those hungry souls without an ounce of emotion driving us. The compassion we would have normally expected and generally common during such ministry times was nowhere to be found. Could we have denied, suppressed, or repressed our underlying feelings? Unnecessary in that those feelings were not only positive but desirable. Was my behavior simply sneaking around that emotion-crushing-beta blocker stifling compassion? Good question, but what about Emily on no medications at all? Could there be another reason?

Let Us Lay a Brief Foundation

In the second chapter of Philippians, after exhorting us to become humble by considering others more important than ourselves, the book's Holy Spirit-inspired author illustrated how Jesus did so: "Though He existed in the form of God, did not consider equality with God something to be grasped but emptied Himself" (Phil. 2:6–7). Of what did the Lord divest Himself to end up a bondservant, then a man, and finally a sacrifice? The Bible states equality with God (i.e., Holy Spirit's attributes and, among them, the compassion driving and empowering Him to perform attesting miracles).

So, let us fast forward to John the Baptist (Matt. 3:13–17) immersing Jesus, whereafter we see Holy Spirit falling upon the Lord. What would that mean? Restoration of His equality with God (i.e., the return of Holy Spirit's attributes, among them compassion to drive and empower Him to perform attesting miracles). Note that Jesus had yet to perform any miracles, signs, or wonders before His baptism. Afterward, He at once went three decisive rounds with Satan, won by a TKO, and drew a line in the sand. Then the Lord went to a wedding at Cana where He publicly revealed His newly recovered supernatural powers, among them compassion, to bless those celebrating a marriage by turning ceremonial water to finest of wine, soon to be followed with an ongoing array of miracles attesting to His divinity.

The Order of Things

Let us first agree: 1) "There is none who do good, no not one" (Ps.14:3); 2) "Every good thing given and every perfect gift is from above" (Jam. 1:17); 3) "and behold the heavens were opening and He saw the Spirit of God descending as a dove and settling upon Him" (Matt. 3:16); 4) "Do you not know that your body is a temple of the Holy Spirit that is within you, whom you have from God, and you are not your own" (1 Cor. 6:19); and 5) "for apart from Me you can do nothing" (John 15:5b). So, isn't it fair to expect that our indwelling Holy Spirit is both the origin and expression of true compassion through believers to conduct Spirit-led ministry? So, when we experience true compassion, does it arise from a human soul? Can our flesh take credit? No.

Years ago, my spiritual father taught this order of things from the pulpit: fact, then faith, then feeling. Reminder of this sequence helps clarify the true source and purpose of compassion. When Holy Spirit's compassion arises in us to act (fact), and we believe and obey His unction to act (faith), then He will pour out compassion through us to others (feeling) to bring change and glory to the Father. As vessels poured out, if we do not feel compassion, that does not deny compassion's presence but may reveal an obstacle within us blocking us from feeling that godly empowered emotion: maybe medication, mental illness, various sins (unbelief, disobedience, judgment, unforgiveness, bitterness, rage, impurity, and on and on), deception, fatigue, sickness, or even demonic oppression. Maybe we have resisted, denied, quenched, grieved, blasphemed, lied to, or insulted the Spirit of Grace, causing Him to sit down.

The absence of our feeling of compassion demands a personal inventory, which may be self-evident or not, but outside today's discussion. However, if we do not feel His compassion, does it mean He has not met His goal? No. Look, the proof of the pudding is in the eating. The litmus test must be this: Are people receiving ministry and manifesting physical or inner healing, deliverance, or answered prayer? If so, then Holy Spirit has achieved His purpose through us as conduits whether we feel His river of compassion or not. Holy Spirit's innate compassion moves Him to minister through us, depends upon our willingness to be His conduits, but is no guarantee we will feel anything. Jesus felt compassion and fed the five thousand. Note: The disciples were merely obedient go-betweens enjoying the ride.

What to Do

So, let me ask: "If you walked in my shoes, would you stop the beta blocker, suffer potential angina, accept a 50 percent increase in risk for another heart attack and death, or continue, like me, not only to steward your heart's health with medication to extend your days of service to the Lord but in so doing, accept a limited or absent sense of His compassion as you minister?"

Let us go one giant step further: "Would you choose to believe that Holy Spirit within you is in charge and will minister compassionately through you to others if you are open, willing, and obedient as a vessel broken and poured out; could it be that ministry is not dependent on whether you feel the Lord's compassion in the process but rather that someone else is touched by the Master's hand? If we are dead to self, would it even matter?"

Postscript

After that Sunday's Kiss from Heaven, I concluded this: Jesus can use us to bless others and glorify Father whether we are feeling emotionally charged or hardened, cold, distant, in despair, or numb to it all. It is about our willingness to let Him work in and through us as vessels on behalf of others, not how our souls feel about it. Remember Jesus saying, "If any man would come after Me, let him deny himself, pick up his cross (truly the zenith of compassion with no fuzzy feelings) and follow Me" (Matt. 16:24). That verse does not focus on how we feel about it, does it? But it confirms we are to consider others more important than ourselves (Phil. 2:3) and, when the Spirit moves, and as the Nike commercial has preached for decades, "Just do it!"

Or, maybe we should merely consider even more venerable words: "Trust in the Lord with all your heart, and do not lean on your own understanding. Acknowledge Him in all your ways, and He will direct your path" (Prov. 3:5–6). Of one thing we can be certain: When we feel compassion, it is the Lord letting us know He plans to include us in His work. If we feel little or only see Him touching others through us, we may be confident that He is at work and has privileged us to come alongside. In either case, it is all about Him and His ways.

QUESTION: Where is the Kiss from Heaven in this God Story?

ANSWER: What a dichotomy! But what a learning experience. You really needed to be there both in our bodies and as a part of the scene near the altar with that hungry bunch of believers to understand. Laying hands on those folks without a wisp of compassion while simultaneously weeping vociferously and praying in an unknown tongue to see folks receive and fall out in the Spirit was close to an out-of-body experience. When Holy Spirit let us in on His well-guarded secret (at least to us) that He (and He alone) is compassion and shares with us as He sees fit (and usually with grace and abandon), it not only made sense but became a Kiss from Heaven. Isn't it wonderful to know that He is the source of compassion, that we don't have to depend upon ourselves but can count on Him alone to minister through us (while blessing us with those good feelings along the way as He chooses)? Doesn't that thought take away pressure when we are not at the top of our game and wishing we could pass the torch when feeling like a "Zippo" with no lighter fluid? It didn't then, but sure does now. Amen.

The Blue Shirts (2011)

The first decade of the new millennium had ended when world-renowned evangelist Rodney Howard Brown, knee-deep in a move of Holy Spirit where hundreds were coming to Christ in Tampa, Florida, pardoned himself to take leave for a brief visit to our little church in Oregon. Wow, I thought, how had our pastor pulled that one off? What an honor and what an opportunity. The leadership of the church then set out to grease our town's evangelical skids to show Rodney we were ready as well for a Holy Spirit move of our own. With Carl Madison, a fiery young evangelist from our own flock, leading the way and after tons of encouragement and training, the church set the Saturday morning preceding Rodney's arrival as D-Day, a time to evaluate our readiness and hone our newly acquired skills as fishers of men. It made perfect sense to have soul-winning testimonies and a handful of newly saved saints to illustrate our readiness to reap the harvest when sharing with our distinguished guest when he arrived. That would bolster Rodney's confidence in what we were already expecting from our budding prowess as evangelists. As you may have concluded, we were a tad premature in our self-congratulatory state.

Preparing the Way

By the time that Saturday rolled around (when we Christian soldiers were to march onward into battle), my wife, Emily, and I had dutifully memorized our cut-to-the-chase laminated plastic Rodney Brown soul-winner card, which led with, "Hello, if you died today, are you sure that you would go to Heaven?" and finished, if things went well, with a gold-plated guarantee you would. Next, we worked on our presentation's phraseology, emphasis, and body language. Then came sincerity, pregnant pausing, and leaning in. Finally, as icing on our evangelical cake, we learned to sweeten our breath, smile when we talked (not that easy), and look our quarry straight in the eye without a blink. Isn't it easy to understand how, in our shared whimsy, we might have felt slightly overconfident in taking on this quest for the kingdom of God?

Looking back, if this means anything, we were as prepared as any uninitiated soul seekers who had never done cold-call evangelism in any part of town, let alone that part of town where two "alleged" cults, both known for their own well-oiled and active evangelical machines, were staring each other down from opposite sides of the same street. Who would be foolhardy enough to dispatch green-neophyte-Christian-evangelistas into those fortified strongholds without a little backup? Someone in scheduling had forgotten to "Remember the Alamo." Anyway, knowing what we now know, had the likes of Joshua's army and Jehoshaphat's angels been available, we might have upgraded the success potential for that day's battle plan to a definite maybe.

So, it was not until Emily and I were deep into Saturday morning's crusading, somewhere between the yin and the yang of storming those fortified gates and being soundly repulsed by them, that we discovered this universal truth: The battle belongs to the Lord—but only if it is on His schedule. In the space of very few moments after the bugle blew, our whimsy flew, and our confidence had withered to that of a couple of ants facing the Nephilim. That may seem hyperbolic, but honestly, dear friend, you were not there.

Battle Call

So, tell us, Lord Jesus, how would you approach a docile middle-aged woman lounging comfortably beneath the mighty appendages of a giant spread-eagle oak in a sun-drenched park on an impeccable Oregon spring morning? Gently, with respect and sincerity, correct? That would always be You, Lord. Well, then, how would You extend her an opportunity to enter an eternal love relationship with Yourself, the kindest, most unselfish and encouraging person who ever traveled this planet? Gently, with respect and sincerity and by using Your cut-to-the-chase plastic laminated Rodney Howard Brown soul-winner card. Well, You, Lord, might keep the card in reserve.

So, how does one, our Blessed Redeemer, reconcile Emily's and my gentle, respectful, and sincere (but laminated) approach to a sudden Hiroshima-like mushroom cloud of abusive hateful insults to the God of our fathers and an unexpected Vesuvius-like lava-laced eruption of vile, vicious, in-your-face verbal abuse of His followers as being inconsiderate, insufferable, invasive, and hypocritical assailants of her privacy.

Want to know something, Lord? We were no more ready than the sons of Sceva (Acts 19:14–16) for that assault or the ensuing line of excuses that morning (e.g., "Oh, my husband would never allow me to do that!") or snubs or draperies pulled or doors hermeneutically sealed that followed in that one neighborhood. Well, it was what it had become, and after two-plus hours, we abandoned our battle plan. Were we in retreat? Emily and I would have preferred to call it a strategic withdrawal, but yes, we were in retreat. Okay, more like the Six-Day War retreat. But it was what it discouragingly was.

Rather than chancing a reenactment of the biblical stoning of the Apostle Paul outside Lystra with Emily and I sharing the featured role, we let caution give way to haste while looking to regroup in the safety of a new venue, a larger park in the northern part of town. Populated on sunny spring weekends by sweet little kids and their trendy soccer moms, we knew the sidelines would be packed with folks enjoying their favorite recreational pastime. Careful reconnaissance of our destination revealed no spread-eagle oaks or anyone basking beneath them. Relieved, we went to work.

The Agony of Defeat

A wall-to-wall festival filled the park with happy people at different events, displays, and snack shacks. This, we agreed, was infinitely more to our liking and, from the beginning, met our comfort levels. We Christians like our comforts, don't we? From that point on, we worked that friendly crowd from stem to stern, worked it hard and repeatedly. Still, the only real harvest we stumbled upon was being gathered by a teenage girl with an imposing anointing steadily bringing her peers, one by one, to Jesus. How we admired her. Regrettably, hours later, our experience had been an altogether dissimilar one; we remained (lacking a better word) skunked. Oh, not that we had not presented the gospel to the folks who would listen. Unfortunately, none took the bait. Fishers of men we were. Fish in our net, there were not. Soon enough, we noted with resignation that the day had slipped away and the hour of our return to the church for debriefing on final approach.

Using a shortcut through the deepening shadows of an earlier raucous but now idle soccer field to reach our parked car felt more like our second retreat of the day. We were not just discouraged but hot, tired, dirty, thirsty, and did I mention . . . assuredly late. In character, Holy Spirit took this interlude to speak: "I want you to return to your car using the sidewalk the same way you came into the park."

"Here we go," I mused inwardly, "another divine intercept and, this time, a real interruption." Knowing better than to question, object, complain, or test Him for an explanation and, as defeated and empty-handed as we were, I knew He had something in mind to redeem the day. He always did when choosing inconvenient stuff like this.

"Emily," I called ahead to where my wife was leaving me far behind while pressing eagerly forward toward a fantasy encounter with our air-conditioned vehicle, "we need to turn around and return by the sidewalk." Fantasy dissolving, Emily did a crisp military "to the rear march" without a word. Wondering how she learned that snazzy move, we soon found that our designated exit from the park was heavily lined on either side by scads of booths and clogged with people conversing with merchants hawking their goods and slowing our progress.

The Thrill of Victory

Weaving our way among the throng of noisy humanity, a male voice rose above the din in a full shout: "Hey, buddy, what are the blue shirts all about?" Emily stopped; I followed. Now, need I remind you I was a seventy-two-year-old male heart patient who was tired, dirty, thirsty, hot, discouraged, late, and assuredly not feeling like anyone's "buddy." Truthfully, the thought annoyed me. What a conundrum! Here we were tardy to a required meeting but sensing Holy Spirit was on the move and, beyond all reason, with a wise guy. Still, there was no choice, was there? Marines would have called it a "column right" when Emily and I executed a crisp, choreographed right-angle turn to confront two rather scruffy young men standing behind the counter of a booth selling subscriptions to a local newspaper. Two more steps put us face-to-face. Cutting to the chase without my laminated card, I blurted, "If I tell you why we are wearing these blue shirts, will you listen to us?" Hearing those few near-testy words brimming with all the stress, fatigue, bodily discomfort, disappointment, and pressure to get back to the church I was carrying, one thing was certain: In no way did that sound like I was greeting a "buddy."

"Sure," both young men echoed happily and in unison. Taken aback by their cheerful response, I rapidly shared the shirts, whose bold white letters wistfully announced today's yet realized "Christian Awakening," a legal mandate by the State of Oregon to help the government restrain Christians from ambushing innocent, unaware citizens and kidnapping them into the kingdom of God against their will. (Did that sound a tad like sarcasm? Astute and true.)

Then I heard myself asking, "Are you ready to listen?"

"Sure," both echoed again in happy unison.

Now, I was more than surprised. How about astounded? Mechanically, I cut again to the chase, regurgitating Rodney's laminated plastic message by memory in record time while finishing with the obligatory, "Are you ready to ask Jesus into your hearts and receive Him as your Lord and Savior?" Okay, my duty was done. Time to boogie.

"Sure," both echoed one more time in even happier unison.

Now, I am bewildered. In the silence of a pregnant pause, here were my thoughts: "Come on, Lord; we work hard, get beat up, dirty, tired, discouraged and, yes, skunked. And then You show up, show off, and 'poof,' two unbelievers saved. What's that all about?"

Well, Emily and I knew what it was about, that old familiar scripture defining this rock and roll day from the beginning, "the battle belongs to the Lord" (1 Sam. 17:47). It was up to Him, and He won that battle when, where, and how He wished.

So, we took advantage of another pregnant pause to pray the young men into the kingdom of Heaven, invite them to a church service, encourage them to buy a Bible, find a baptismal tank, and, finally, lay hands upon them to impart a blessing and hopefully an anointing from Holy Spirit. And to our surprise, which was no surprise, all with adequate time to make our scheduled debriefing.

The Brief Debrief

"Yes, two," I recall hearing my voice rise, but this time to our evangelist leader's request for a "spiritual body count" (i.e., those "saved" on our outing). Proudly responding by holding two victorious fingers aloft, Emily and I both knew that we were taking credit where credit was not due. So, we apologized to the Lord, gave Him all the glory, thanked him for a day's effort not spent in vain, for faithfully executing His Word (although taking His sweet time about it), for two new saints in the kingdom, and another "Kiss from Heaven."

Looking around, Emily was gone, overcome by the resurrected fantasy of her soon-to-be air-conditioned nap. In full agreement, I chased her down. It had been a long, long day.

Postscript

If you are not aware, those seven sons of Sceva (Acts 19:14–16) were allegedly exorcists for a high priest, their father. Have you, as I have, wondered if they were not just enthusiastic young wannabees trying to imitate Dad or mimic Jesus for a little entertainment? You know kids. Was it trendy throughout the youth culture at the time for kids to impersonate Jesus, pretending to manifest His powers by using His name and imitating His behavior, like superhero adulation for the younger generation of our day? Don't you remember having your Superman cape, one of Mom's best towels safety-pinned to the shoulders of your shirt, and crying, "Up, up and away!" before leaping off the porch roof to gravity's "down, down to stay" and, without saying, an unexpectedly unpleasant earthy greeting? Like Superman (or Spiderman et al. in these days of the Marvel comic's bunch revival), might Jesus have been the most famous "superhero" in His? Wouldn't you have wanted to see His miracles as a kid in those days and then emulate them? Wouldn't you like to see them today? Ask any deliverance minister. Anyway, the results of our using the name of Jesus in Saturday morning's evangelistic thrust, honest as it was, and the Sceva boys' ministry were both beyond unimpressive. While ours became a little "heated," theirs, if you take time to read the scripture (Acts 19:14–16), became a tad "chilly." Then there was Simon the sorcerer trying to buy Holy Spirit to gain personal fame. Peter had to rebuke him (Acts 8:9–25) for using the name of Jesus to enhance his own reputation. Similar willingness to misuse the name of Jesus in the Christian community for entertainment or to gather personal power, fame, or money persists to the present if you have not noticed.

The Name of Jesus

Using the name of Jesus in self-serving ways will always bring setbacks, no matter what your spiritual persuasion. "God is not mocked; for whatever a man sows, this he will also reap. For the one who sows to his own flesh shall from the flesh reap corruption" (Gal. 6:7–9). To even trifle with the name of Jesus for self-interest or self-indulgence has brought folks to their knees and, stunningly, not in a holy way. Consider the televangelists of the 1980s, high-visibility pastors over the past decades, and leaders in local churches who have fallen by exploiting the name of Jesus for their own benefit. Using Jesus' name cavalierly to lift "self" up has often brought the "cavalier" down.

Why? Because the name of Jesus is a holy name. In the name of Jesus is all that He is and all that He does. Commonly, we use His name to finish our prayers: "We pray all this in Jesus' name." What are we asking but for Holy Spirit to conduct only what Jesus would or could do because of who He is, our all-powerful Lord and Savior. To ensure those prayers are holy, filtered of any sinful or selfish intention, and fit for Father's ears, we may pray in the Spirit—He who knows how and what to pray when we do not (Rom. 8:26)—so they may arrive in Father's throne room without edit.

Misusing the Name

We often wonder if God answers our prayers. Sadly, what we often experience is a "no" response because we ask amiss to spend the fruit on our own indulgences (James 4:3). Jesus never sought self-gratification (e.g., entertainment, merchandise, power, fame, or money) at the Father's expense or to glorify Himself ("If I glorify Myself, My glory is nothing" (John 8:54). He had no fleshly lusts because He was a sinless, pure, and other-centered servant ("For even the Son of Man did not come to be served, but to serve" (Mark 10:45). He looked only to glorify His Father, serve others, and never Himself ("I go to the Father. And whatever you ask in My name, that I will do, that the Father may be glorified in the Son" (John 14:12–13).

Again, notice the intention to glorify the Father, serve others, and not Himself. Using the name of Jesus can get to be dicey, can't it? How? Well, He is the person with all the resources, power, abilities, and gifts. Haven't we read that without Him, we can do nothing (John 15:5), but with Him, all things are possible (Phil. 4:13)? So, do we have the hubris to think that we can manipulate, control, and use the name of Jesus to selfishly have our way, fill our own wants, and give us His glory? Both the sons of Sceva and Simon the Sorcerer exuded that attitude. (Parenthetically, even Superman never has. Think about it.) Talk about vanity.

Vanity

Look, God tells us not to use His name in vain (Ex. 20:7). One interpretation of the word "vain" is pursuing a self-centered course of thought or action for our own benefit. Should we ever use the name of Jesus in prayer (or elsewise) to satisfy our own vain desires? Never. Should we even pray for ourselves? Is that praying amiss? Not if it is according to His will to keep us from temptation, deliver our hearts from evil, fill us with His Spirit, revere and obey Him, or please Him to bring Father glory.

Proper Prayer

Prayer is never meant to control (denying another's free will or insuring our own) but to love (sacrificially devoted to the good of another or denying ourselves on their behalf). We are not meant to walk competitively (striving and driving) with one another or on eggshells (tentatively and anxiously) with God but instead selflessly with others and in holy fear (grand respect, love, and obedience) with Father. Jesus says it all, "Greater love has no one than this, that one lay down his life for his friends (John 15:13)" and "If you love Me, you will keep My commandments" (John 14:15). It is all about others-centered love.

When we use His name boldly in prayer, revering Him and His will while considering others more important than ourselves, it is always a win-win event that pleases and honors the Father while blessing others. Good stuff happens, and both Heaven and Earth benefit.

Anyway, that's why Emily and I often pray in the Spirit (who knows how to pray when we don't) and prefer divine intercepts where Holy Spirit takes command, makes all the plans, does all the work, blesses who He chooses, and gives Father all the glory. We get the privilege to go on the journey surrendered, committed, and obedient as devoted servants to do what we must to see others loved and God get the glory. That makes pleasing the Father seem like a walk in the park, doesn't it? At least on that Saturday afternoon where Father was pleased and received the glory when two living souls chose Him over this world, made His day, enshrined theirs, and brought ours a "Kiss from Heaven."

QUESTION: Where is the Kiss from Heaven in this God Story?

ANSWER: I have a note stuck to our refrigerator that states: (1) Live in the now, (2) Stay in your lane, and (3) Bloom where you're planted. I am not sure when I penned that heavy-duty nugget of wisdom, but it may have arisen as a Phoenix from the smoldering ruins of that Saturday morning's evangelical holocaust in the southern part of Albany and the onset of my brief encounter with PTSD (poetic exaggeration). When sharing this story, I try to take the high road by crediting Holy Spirit for rescuing the rest of that day, those two scruffy young men virtually choosing their own salvations as we left the park, and then our taking the credit due at the meeting. (I know, I know . . . wretched man that I am.)

The Remnant (2010)

Sadly, and recently, my oldest friend and most enduring, if not most endearing, friendship (dating from shared side-by-side cradles in the final year of the 1930s) had both come to tragic ends following his valiant but futile battle with lung cancer. Emily and I had flown east from Oregon to pay tribute at his memorial service and were ferrying my beloved but elderly 1991 Isuzu Trooper back to the West Coast. Traveling the New York State Thruway west of Buffalo, out of the blue (a rare condition for any Buffalo sky), the inner voice of Holy Spirit spoke: "Go to Missouri. A man is struggling, and I want to help him."

"Missouri in the summer?" my own inner voice was quick to moan. Why the whining? Well, I had intentionally avoided meeting anyone in St. Louie, Louie, since the summer of 1972. Who could forget the sole air conditioner in our family's spanking new Volvo station wagon suddenly capitulating to the torrid heat of a Missouri August while giving up the ghost and its only purpose for taking up space on this planet? Who could forget being trapped in that bright yellow overheated oven, windows flung wide in futility, crammed with one-half-dozen hyperhidrotic (supersaturated sweat-soaked) half-naked humans and one longhaired slobbering dog? Who could forget helplessly watching one another suffer near-heatstroke in a losing battle with that unmerciful St. Louis summer heat spell?

Those not-so-easily-forgettable memories, dear Christian, I guarantee surfaced nowhere near the vicarious misery in you today as that day of infamy imposed on our family during that epic journey through the "Show Me" state in the steamy summer of seventy-two. So, with sacred solemnity (I am alliterating for emphasis), I vociferously vowed no one in that day's Trooper travel would be suddenly subjected to those kinds of "Volvorian" vicissitudes again. (Okay, I overdid it.)

The Where, What, Why, When, and Who in Missouri

For Pete's sake, who was this man for whom Emily and I, and for PETA's sake, do not forget Daisy the dog, were to face certain dehydration and risk serious heat-induced medical maladies? For a fact, neither of us knew one soul from Missouri (well, there was my Marine brother Pete from Columbia) until Emily recalled a man who spoke at our fellowship in Oregon months earlier.

Then, I, too, sort of remembered: This summer, Emily recalled, a grand "intercessorama" (a Google search revealed it as the "Wilderness Outcry") in Poplar Bluff, Missouri, promised to draw over a hundred thousand saints eager to pray for our nation. Pressing our veteran Tom-Tom into service gave us two days' doable "down and distance." No further argument followed from this man when clear that our new adventure would take us nowhere near that cauldron called St. Louis.

Our interstate journey south from Erie, Pennsylvania, to Poplar Bluff was an uneventful trek for which to be thankful, considering the old girl had over 220,000 miles on her chassis and no history of exercise for an entire year. (For clarity and my safety's sake—if you get my drift—we are talking the Isuzu trooper here.) Settled the following afternoon in a "Bluff" motel, Emily and I discovered a weekly worship service for those laboring long hours to prepare for this summer's prayer vigil would be held in a local facility, the Gamma Health Services Convention Center, that evening. By then, we were rested and ready to crash that party to see what the Lord had in store; it did not take long.

A Divine Appointment

Toward the meeting's end, a generous man in his late fifties came forward, suggesting all in attendance gather in line across the front of the "sanctuary" for prayer. Assume I did, and correctly so, this was the effort's leader, a local businessman and farmer, Jerry Murphy. The prayer line, stretching from one side of the cavernous center to the other, featured the man himself already laying on hands as we took our places. Emily and I, as we often do, prepared by holding hands as a couple. Barely had Jerry Murphy laid one hand apiece upon us when he suddenly pitched backward two steps, a reaction not dissimilar to simultaneously touching each pole of an open 110 Volt circuit. His shocked expression, matching our own, I suspect, quickly morphed into one layered with curiosity. Eyes narrowed, with a leader's quiet authority, he demanded, "Who are you, and why are you here?" and further on that evening: "Are you here for my restoration?" Emily and I exchanged smiles. Holy Spirit was wasting precious little time.

The Leader

Jerry Murphy was an enigma, if not a contradiction, a down-home boy in a big city suit. In time, we discovered he was born a dirt-poor farmer, graduated a microbiologist, transformed himself into an industrious entrepreneur and owner of multiple companies, and, as the local folks said, had deep pockets, especially among the Christian community. Yet, around his 440-acre Moriah ranch, Jerry appeared as the poster child for America's successful ranchers while, paradoxically, at the next moment, rubbing Brooks Brother's shoulders with nationally respected businesspeople, politicians, and church leaders.

He seemed to have met everyone that came up in a conversation while privately guarding his family and, most recently, his grandbabies. To his grandsons' delight, Jerry had a generous part of Kubota's entire orange earth-moving inventory (later to morph into a field of John Deere green) mimicking an oversized Tonka collection. To no one's surprise, the man "flew" each piece with the dispatch of a sure-handed aviator, another skill he had long ago mastered from the 87-mile-per-hour Piper Cub to the 1470-mile-per-hour McDonnell Douglas F-4 Phantom.

Jerry Murphy cherished the precious 440 acres of ranchland that he had roamed as a child (and bought as an adult to build a home and create a ranch) as sacred ground to be nurtured, farmed, and protected as he would any vulnerable family member. That would have included his prize bulls, a growing Angus herd, a scattering of horses, and all thirteen free-range donkeys along the way.

People agreed that the man was undoubtedly a hail fellow well met but also a take-charge leader who got things done. No surprise that others often called Moriah to ally or partner themselves with Jerry when seeking help in uncontrollable circumstances or to explore fertile business opportunities. Then, his reputation had grown in the church as a man with a gift of teaching financial accountability, growth, and stewardship through personal and formal meetings (later extended into television's "God TV" and streaming his own Moriah weekly program around the planet).

Recently, the man had become a familiar figure in the American Church by joining two nationally known church leaders promoting an upcoming summer's prayer vigil on the ranch. The meeting was open to the world and would supply camping, water, showers, waste facilities, and intermittent food to lend support to this grand venture. Long-term unselfish funding for various non-profits and other-centered ways to help the afflicted and the needy had long ago elevated Jerry Murphy in the hearts of those who knew him. Other times, his visibility did quite the opposite. This was to be one of those "other times." Ironically, Murphy's Law* was about to raise its ugly head.

The General

Somewhere along the way, someone tagged Jerry with the nickname "General." He enjoyed it and considered it a humorous and backhanded compliment by his competitors on the one hand but, on the other, due recognition for his status as an astute business tactician and respected leader among his peers, associates, and employees on the other. The man also understood at one level that any new acquaintance might construe him a retired military officer, a misnomer and way he never referred to himself. Nor did he see the need to clarify the handle, General, when harmlessly used by others. It was a nickname, for heaven's sake. He was no more a formal Unites States military general than was Harland Sanders, the Kentucky Fried Chicken giant, a United States military colonel. For both men, those titles were merely familiarities. For Jerry Murphy, that was about to change. **

No Good Deed Goes Unpunished

Without warning and in the twinkling of an eye, there came this tempest in a teapot-turned-boiling internet inferno, where naysayers and critics erupted like Vesuvius spewing murderous lava over the internet. Overnight, green-eyed God-haters and jealous foes of Jerry's highly promoted Christian prayer gathering, along with hordes of small-minded social media pot stirrers, began public smear campaigns challenging not only Jerry's nickname "General" but, more so, his alleged lack of candor by not being upfront about his lack of past military service to the public.

"Isn't it larceny for a civilian with no military service to assume a general officer's rank to identify himself?" they cried. "Isn't it illicit or, if not, then, at the very least, unethical?" Not just a handful wondered: "How can we trust a duplicitous man with the spiritual authority to lead Christians into prayer for our struggling nation?" Within days, his accusers were publicly trashing his character and questioning his moral right to act on behalf of America to pray for anything. Jerry Murphy should step aside, suggested the self-appointed internet judges.

Predictably, the firestorm that mounted from afar ignited local tinder who took opportunity to settle old grudges or fan more recent accusations to fuel the blaze. Sooner than later, as near as one could discover, except for a scant few of the Poplar Bluff's seventy-plus pastors and their church bodies, a greater share of the remaining Christian community had turned sour with the ensuing summer's event or were frankly calling for its cancelation. What a sad and humiliating mess.

Facing Facts

As we finished breakfast at the local Perkins restaurant the following Monday morning, dark principalities way beyond the ordinary were engaged to destroy the upcoming summer prayer event along with this man's reputation. If we do not understand why negative surface events are happening, it is often because their genesis hides cocooned in darkness. When we penetrate darkness with light, that would be lies with truth, we will always uncover one form or another of deception (practices like pretense, illusion, subterfuge, treachery, perversion, delusion, jealousy, or betrayal), which is the single remaining arrow in our enemy's quiver since the cross.

So, when invited to join a meeting with Jerry's trusted staff later that morning, the "General" proposed a letter be emailed to each of the city's pastors. In it he openly regretted his willingness to let others

call him "General" and publicly clarified he was not a military veteran. Personally, I felt him a little self-deprecating while Emily and
I both wondered why Jerry fell short of explaining why he had not
embraced this nickname, "General," as a symbol of appreciation and
respect in his heart from those around him. Who wouldn't value that
treatment, and what pastor (or any red-blooded American) would not
be humbled by it?

Pressed by Holy Spirit, it was necessary to take a risk: "Jerry, a
letter is too impersonal; you must go face-to-face with these pastors."
Everyone in the room agreed, "Don't send the letter; go in person."
Jerry relented, although reluctantly. Emily and I took his pregnant
pause as a deeper struggle.

And The Truth Will Set You Free

We asked for a time of ministry. Jerry agreed, and within a day,
we met. Others had misunderstood this whole tempest in a
teapot-turned-tornado, blew it out of proportion, and provoked vin-
dictive responses by still more people who weaponized the attacks out
of their own stuff. We see this mob effect routinely on social media,
where people dog pile on others about situations of which they know
little but use as opportunity to voice an opinion and feel heard. It soon
became clear, at least to Emily's and my hearts, who was wearing the
white hat here and who had the "issues."

We had met Jerry only hours before. Although a bigger-than-life
target, he had no agenda aside from the one published, "Wilderness
Outcry." As so often happens, Holy Spirit had sent us to help rescue
another saint from themselves and the mob about them. Thankfully,
and as usual, Jesus had a plan.

Observing a ministry recipient's privacy (mandated in any arena
of restoration), let us first be clear: Every human on God's green
earth deals with one level or another of residual childhood distress.
Commonly, innocent youngsters who suffer through perceived or

actual negative experiences of abuse or neglect misinterpret those traumatic circumstances in ways that influence how they believe and feel about themselves as individuals. Usually, those misinterpretations are lies, accepted as truth we believe wholeheartedly, to which we respond with negative emotion, behave irrationally, and consequently end by punctuating our lives with times of substantial regrets.

In a comparable way to early trauma in all our lives, our new friend's unique childhood experience had given birth to a belief engendering an emotional Achilles heel, a false belief lived as truth which ended up an obstacle. Then, as ministry progressed, Holy Spirit's impartation of His truth set the "General" free from that lie. Finally, with the Spirit sharing our new friend's identity in God's eyes (and quickly his own), a freedom arose to confront his difficult present-day circumstances through his new lenses of truth. Would a change in behavior follow? We expected so.

With energy, enthusiasm, and faith we rarely see, our friend set out in his newly found truth to humbly meet the town's pastors, face-to-face and one at a time. Day by day, he would report: "I went to clarify and repent of my past behavior and, invariably, those pastors* ended up sharing similar repentance with me. I found that, at the end of each meeting, I had been forgiven in each pastor's sight while I had, in turn, forgiven them."

All Things Work Together

Meanwhile, convinced that he had to intervene personally in this now-nationwide whirlwind, one of Jerry's well-known partners in this effort came to hold a group problem-solving session with the local pastors. Things went well in the already primed pastoral community, who agreed to support or at least not hinder the upcoming summer's event. Strangely, shortly thereafter, that partner retreated by email from his future obligations (for reasons unknown to Emily and me) and backed out of the whole shebang. This left Jerry holding an enormous bag of time, money, and energy spent and even bigger decisions to make.

The now not-so-latent "General" in Jerry, I discovered, had long before conferred with the Lord on how to make those decisions. It was now clear that by heavenly default, God had promoted the man as His general for this season and, as his assigned mission, a true remnant (what remains of a community after it undergoes a catastrophe according to the "Anchor Dictionary"), and now the fondest dream of Jerry Murphy's summer.

Emily and I left, prepared to return to Missouri and a gathering of that God-filtered holy remnant now in the hands of Jesus and safe from the hands of inscrutable men. And sure enough, that summer, just shy of a thousand faceless but fervent Bible-believing saints from over thirty-two states and six countries gathered along gently moving Indian Creek, winding its way through a cushion of verdant meadow to pray day and night for God to move across America.

During that summer prayer festival, we, the Jesus remnant, endured heat indexes of over 105 degrees Fahrenheit (triggering memories of St. Louis in me, don't you know) and a microburst wind (a well-timed Holy Spirit metaphor) that lifted our giant tent poles out of their sockets and tent off the ground while sweeping dozens of smaller camping tents into who knows what county. All this occurred, as far as we knew, without one soul murmuring but among billows of ongoing praise. In recent times, had the Lord moved with the intensity, sweetness, mercy, and glory over an entire week like we had enjoyed? Not to Emily's or my recollections since our journey through the 1990s revivals.

Postscript

May I beat a dead horse on your behalf? Thank you. A ship just one degree off course while crossing the Pacific will end up miles away from its intended destination. Do you see that our "General" needed a course correction? Sure, more one-degree course-correcting Kiss from Heaven of truth received from Holy Spirit during his early-morning ministry session brought about the needed change. Wish we had time to describe the General's years since our early days and his apostolic work with the First Nations, mentor to multiple spiritual sons, construction of his well-known and highly used Moriah Ranch prayer altar, growing numbers of Green Tractor podcasts, and the ongoing growth of the ranch's ministry; sadly, that story must wait.

What "kissed" Emily and me about our small part in this whole scenario was how Jesus detoured us, a couple of aging nobodies heading west in their vintage Isuzu Trooper, to instead head south to help a man willing to humble himself and trust the Lord to turn an unforeseen calamity into a glorious celebration. And, as an unsolicited clarification, didn't Holy Spirit's ministry time with the General answer Jerry's lingering question about our visit, "Are you here for my restoration?"

Thinking back, if not to partner with Jesus in His exploits with "General Murphy," would Holy Spirit have rerouted us from Buffalo? What do you think? Then again, that detour may have been as much about releasing my beloved Isuzu Trooper to that baby Christian in recovery and recently released from prison. By the last report, our old silver girl was still running like a top, as was her owner. Kisses from Heaven by the number in this tale, are there not, proving, again, the goodness of God in the land of the living (Ps. 27:13).

* Murphy's Law: Anything that can go wrong will go wrong.

** This ministry has proven of great benefit to pastors and leaders who are open targets for attacks on many fronts in these last days and need a short-term city of refuge where Holy Spirit can bring peace, calm, clarity, and direction to their life in Christ.

QUESTION: What is the Kiss from Heaven in this God Story?

ANSWER: God has a unique way of placing us on His threshing floor to separate the grain from the chaff, doesn't He? In the twinkling of an eye, a grand soon-to-be-celebrated Christianorama of one hundred thousand plus was winnowed to a mere fraction of its predicted self. Ah, but God understands the value of catastrophe, that the holy seed is in the stump (Isa. 6:13), and here as a remnant of God's people set aside as a new beginning. What a Kiss from Heaven for those who survived that heavenly downsizing and prospered by it during a glorious week on Moriah Ranch in the summer of 2010 . . . and for Jerry Murphy, newly promoted general officer in the army of the Lord. Attention on deck, Christian soldiers! Amen.

In His Time (2017)

Three weeks nestled deep among the hardwoods lining the shore of the shiny mirror that is Skaneateles Lake in Upstate New York had been relaxation on steroids. Wrapping up the final day of the loveliest September of a lifetime, Emily and I polished it off with what we loved best, a challenging early-morning walk with Peaches, our five-year-old Jack Russell-Puggle-blend-of-frenzied-chipmunk-ch asing-tousle-headed-hunter-dog, who daily took us to a point beyond breathlessness while climbing the hills and dales of our hardscrabble rural road to its farthest reaches. That would be Peter and Tammy's pasture, populated in 2017 with fewer exquisitely spoiled Arabian mares than in years past. Per usual, a handful of those few happy-go-lucky ladies were more than willing to lumber across their lush green carpet to snatch a handful of "greener" grass pulled from our side of their often pervious and always undecided electric fence, which from time immemorial had kept us guessing but never the horses.

Sprinkled along our journey were on-road chats with ever-diminishing handfuls of aging gray-headed friends gradually replaced by their own multiplying progeny. That growing number of less-familiar faces occupied time and space unconsciously reserved for those sadly passed and now sorely missed ones. After seventy-eight years, this scenario had woefully, but all too suddenly, become a disturbing but irreversible reality. By day's end, this same disturbing but irreversible reality landed smack dab in our own family's lap. Emily had flown to Oregon for sister's week, an annual reunion with her six remaining female siblings, while I packed for my return to Texas. Then, my eldest nephew left a voice message: His brother had passed. Hugh Henry Martin, a good and brave man who carried the first names of both his grandfathers, was pushing into his early fifties. Having endured years of hardship and struggle with chronic illness, Hugh had silently slipped the surly bonds of earth to be with his Lord in the still of the previous night. His immediate family scheduled a memorial service for the following Wednesday at 10:00 a.m. in the distant village of Central Square. Delaying my long trip to Texas for a couple of days, I chose instead to make the shorter one to remember Hugh and help the family celebrate his journey to Jesus. The intervening days passed quickly, filled with last-minute events unworthy of note. That was about to end.

The Best-Laid Plans of Mice and Men

According to my excellent plan, but without consulting even one mouse who brazenly shared our aging summer cottage, I loaded the Toyota. Then, after vacuuming the cabin, scrubbing the kitchen floor, cleaning the refrigerator, bathing Peachy, and washing my dirty clothes and myself, I finished by preparing tomorrow morning's cup of java for the microwave before hitting the hay. Well before the chickens, I arose, deposited a lone remaining bag in the car, locked the out-buildings, and went to grab my missing shaving kit while pausing long enough to place yesterday's prepared coffee mug in the microwave. Programming one minute into the timer while leaving to turn off the water heater, I returned to retrieve my now-steaming java.

Regrettably, that would not be possible. I had incorrectly entered one hour into the microwave's timer, leaving the machine still about its task with considerable time left. To no surprise, but ample annoyance, over half of the giant cup's contents had boiled over into the guts of the microwave mounted above the stove, continued hastily to and through the waiting stovetop where, under the sure grip of gravity, unceremoniously dribbled down its innards as rivulets to flood my newly scrubbed floor. Don't you know that the damage control required by this mishap severely disrupted and changed the precise schedule of my (now) not-so-excellent plan to reach Central Square by 9:50 a.m. The best-laid plans of mice and men ofttimes go astray. No way to blame the mice for this mess.

Poochie and I left the cottage at 8:45 a.m., tardy by one-half an hour, to begin a journey north along the lake on New York Route 41 to mail a package at the UPS store in the village of Skaneateles, another last-minute unintended detour, which further delayed departure from the village until 9:09 a.m. The road leaving the village to the north, New York Route 321, posted a forty-five-mile-per-hour speed limit on the way to its junction with Route 5 East. Now, I feel your drudgery with this prattling tale. Why the need to post all these times, miles, and distances? Why all the math? Why not cut to the chase and get to the church? Have faith; it's all part of the tale, pilgrim. A road map of Onondaga and Oneida counties, if available, would be invaluable (but unnecessary with a good imagination) to your keeping track of this about to be mind-bending journey.

A Brief Pause

Briefly pulling off the highway at the junction of Route 321 and Route 5 East, our GPS added to my rising stress levels. Both the Toyota's clock and my phone read 9:22 a.m. Oh, no! We had thirty-one miles over two more legs to reach the memorial service but only twenty-eight minutes to arrive by 9:50 a.m. A quick mental computation revealed that would take an average speed of over seventy miles per hour to achieve that feat, an impossible task.

The first leg of twelve miles to the Hiawatha Blvd exit off I-690 (get out your map) would take thirteen of those twenty-eight minutes. We would arrive at that exit by 9:35 a.m. with fifteen minutes to cover the second leg, the remaining nineteen miles. Another impossible feat.

Are you keeping up? Hope so.

Stressed over the time deficit while jetting onto Route 5 East, with half a laugh, I murmured aloud, "Lord, if we are going to get to the church on time, somewhere along the way, we will need a little transport." Transport? Remember when the evangelist Phillip left the newly baptized Ethiopian eunuch in a mud puddle only to find himself instantly outside the town of Azotus in Caesarea (Acts 8:39–40)? How about when Jesus and His disciples were riding out one of those nasty storms on the Sea of Galilee before "immediately" finding themselves safe on the far shore (John 6:21)? Yes, like those folks, we would need a little "timely" help on today's journey.

Fine Tuning

Exiting I-690 to enter Hiawatha Blvd, I glanced at the car's clock; then I looked again. Then, I fixated on that instrument. It read 9:24 a.m. Awestruck, I pulled over on the road's shoulder and double-checked my phone's time, 9:24 a.m. No difference. "What, Lord, what? You did it! You transported us twelve miles in two minutes."

Later that day, I went over that leg with further thought. True, we had covered twelve miles in two minutes flat. That was six miles per minute, a 360-miles-per-hour sprint. More likely, however, only the latter ten miles of the leg was "immediate" (as the Bible alludes were both Phillip's and Jesus's instantaneous trips) and followed our first couple miles (using the entire two minutes the leg took), where I distinctly recalled driving at sixty miles per hour. Then, the rate of speed must have instantly increased to infinite over the remaining ten-mile stretch and an immediate arrival at the Hiawatha Blvd. exit, a distance that should have taken eleven minutes at the posted speed limit. Curiously, I had no memory outside that leg's first two miles. Little wonder.

Still with me?

Sitting on the Hiawatha exit from I-690, trying to grasp the consequences of our two-minute dash, I updated our original GPS readings, which had originally projected nineteen miles over fifteen minutes to the church from our present position. But now, with eleven minutes saved by the "transport," the available travel time to the church increased to a full twenty-six minutes to cover those same nineteen miles. Praise Jesus, we were certain to arrive at the church by 9:50 a.m. as planned. True to the GPS, we entered the church parking lot on time (actually, one minute early) after averaging forty-four miles per hour (by a later calculation) instead of over seventy miles per hour originally calculated for a trip over roads dotted with construction and reduced speed zones through the City of Syracuse, Town of Brewerton, and into Central Square.

Later, I checked the math.

As skeptical as you, too, are likely to be, I made certain to repeat that trip before leaving New York for Texas while Emily and I did the same the following year, not once but three times, to confirm or deny the original calculations. The distance over the ground was the same, and the time from the junction of Route 321 and Route 5 East to the exit from I-690 onto Hiawatha Blvd. never varied more than seconds from the thirteen minutes our GPS had predicted before the "transport." The completed construction required a couple minutes less to the church. You may check my math with your phone's GPS or your maps of Onondaga and Oneida Counties in Upstate New York. Little good will it do for doubters, I understand, since this event was exceedingly difficult to put into public print. And I am the person who lived through it, well, along with Peaches, who, although she considers herself a person, is saying nothing. Who can blame her!

A Beautiful Goodbye

The Martin family spent the early minutes gathering before a service highlighted by Hugh's wife Martha's loving testimony describing the couple's married years. It was a poignant goodbye that any Christian husband would cherish and a depth of love that any devoted wife would long to share at her husband's passing. Tears flowed, and the sweet presence of the Lord was deeply reassuring and comforting while Martha spoke. Afterward, I felt confident this Christian woman and her family would conquer their present grief, if only by their faith in Christ. What a glorious day we had celebrating Hugh's homecoming. How encouraging to see faith in action and loved ones resting in an unquestionable dependence on the goodness of God in an age when so many folks struggle. Who could fathom His goodness on that day? That two-minute "transport" made sure I would not squander one minute of that memorial service or, as Hugh's Uncle and the last of my generation in the family, interrupt the importance of Martha's beautiful testimony by being tardy. To the Lord, my presence in the service held something more than I could embrace in that moment. Later, I came to understand when reliving Martha's expression of joy, a Kiss from Heaven for the both of us, when we first met in the chapel on my arrival. We humans often, sadly, underestimate our importance to one another. Evidently, the Lord doesn't.

Postscript

If this tale does not drive our brethren reductionist First Corinthians Chapter 12 crowd to distraction, I do not know what would. More so, I had not even offered an adequate prayer for our brief "transport" but merely reminded the Lord of our dilemma. It later became clear for the family's sake that Jesus felt it important that I be punctual. So, merciful person He is, the Lord intervened to shorten our travel time.

Time travel in the Bible involves both transport and translation; that statement is always subject to debate. Transport, as I understand it, involves instant horizontal movement over the earth, as noted earlier when the Spirit took Phillip to Azotus in Caesarea (Acts 8:39–40) and Jesus with His disciples "immediately" to the shore during a ferocious storm on the Sea of Galilee (John 6:21). Translation, however, is a vertical phenomenon as was Jesus's ascension in a cloud (Acts 1:9), Enoch's being "taken up" (Heb.11:5), and Elijah's chariot ride (2 Kings 2:11). In the latter two examples, those translations were to avoid the vicissitudes of physical death. However, if we read the book of Revelation (11:3), we find two witnesses, thought by a number to be Enoch and Elijah, originally spared through translation by the Lord, finally suffering their physical death. The Bible is clear: "And just as it is destined for a man to die once…" (Heb. 9:27).

Manipulation of time is another fascinating subject the scriptures address. Commonly, questions surrounding this enigma devolve into whether time has moved forward, stood still, or gone in reverse. Hezekiah, granted his request for healing and blessed with fifteen more years, challenged God for a sign to confirm that promise. The Father did so by moving the sun backward while returning its shadow ten steps (degrees) down the stairway of Ahaz as a guarantee and while losing forty minutes in time (2 Kings 20:1–11).

A second instance documents Joshua's "long day" when the Lord delivered the Amorites into Joshua's hands after he had boldly commanded both the sun and moon to stop in space, giving him time to crush his foe. So, there was no movement of those bodies for about a day (twenty-three hours and twenty minutes to be exact), which gave Israel ample time to take full revenge on its enemy (Joshua 10:12–14). Much professionally written theory and opinion has sought to explain these changes over centuries with inevitable ongoing residual disagreement and rare consensus on how we may account for those lost twenty-four hours. Okay, we have time backing up in Hezekiah's case, standing still in Joshua's, and folks like Phillip, Jesus and the disciples, and Peaches and me transcending time. Who can understand this? It can be uncomfortable. Are we done now, you ask? No, we have yet to serve this curious banquet's glorious dessert.

The late Reverend Bob Curry, a pastor-evangelist-missionary -mentor and friend for over thirty years experienced a perilously low fuel state with a gauge on "empty" while driving his family through Death Valley, true double jeopardy as it was in the dead of night with no gas stations within reach. Without warning, their car plunged into triple jeopardy, a brief but anxiety-provoking season of total blackness with no visible road until the vehicle broke out in a mountain descent on a highway leading to the arms of a gas station outside Bakersfield, California, an immediate "transport" of over two hundred miles.

Whoa, that was one colossal Kiss from Heaven and a place where greater faith was born, wouldn't you think? Well, only if you believe it. What is your opinion about this stuff, dear Christian? Are you still with us? Finding it a stretch? Given up on the math? To this day that unscheduled transport on the way to Central Square stretches my flesh but simultaneously builds my faith. Then, consider this: Didn't Jesus say we would not only do what he did but even greater things (John 14:12)?

Okay, the transport for Jesus and the disciples was less than eight miles across the Sea of Galilee, probably ten miles for Peaches and me on the trip to Central Square, thirty miles to Azotus for Phillip and, for our friend's family, a whopping two hundred miles across the dark desert through the mountains to a gas station on the way downhill toward Bakersfield. He is the "same yesterday, today, and forever" (Heb. 13:8), isn't He? Sometimes even greater.

So, if you choose to call all those transports "greater things," then, beyond a shadow of any doubt, this entire tale becomes a Kiss from Heaven.

QUESTION: Where is the Kiss from Heaven in this God Story?

ANSWER: When aviators catapulted from the USS Independence in A-4E Skyhawk buddy tankers at night in the mid-1960s, their planes reached 170 knots of airspeed over three hundred feet. During that ride, G-forces drove the lens in both eyes toward their retinas, making those pilots legally blind for about two seconds. Those two seconds of blurred red vision while leaving the bow of a ship at 170 knots a mere sixty feet above the water placed that aviator figuratively in the hands of God. Sometimes figuratively turned, actually, when a plane went vertical, requiring a negative G pushover to stay flying. Then, that bird would disappear below the carrier's bow until it gained enough speed to climb, its lights slowly gaining altitude ahead of the ship. Infrequently, the plane and pilot suffered an unintended ditch and loss of life. G-forces can be tricky on land or sea. Can you imagine traveling (being translated) ten statute miles over zero seconds at infinite speed in a Toyota Camry? Those G-forces would have blinded us, crushed the vehicle, and ruined everyone's day . . . had there been time. Happily, there wasn't. Now, there's a Kiss from Heaven which not only built my faith in Jesus but, for certain, sold me on that Camry.

Afterthoughts

I, Caleb, the storyteller and eyewitness in this book, am concerned that I have not adequately conveyed to my readers an unshakable understanding that Father is unrelenting to reveal His active presence in our lives, to keep us engaged in our relationship with Him and that His inexpressible goodness and kindness is always working to exchange His beauty for the ashes in our lives (Isa. 61:3).

Dear Christian, consider how many opportunities each of us has missed to become part of God's divine works, all because we were distracted and driven by the lures of this world, the subtle whispers of our enemy, or the persistent cravings of our insatiable flesh. Or, as we repeatedly have shown here, by being unaware of the Lord in our midst while failing to seek His intervention. Were we all willing to set aside but a small part of our daily consciousness to become ever-ready watchmen on His wall, waiters at His table, or on-call first responders to His every need, how much more might our lives be of use to bring Father glory and honor due His name by praying to glorify His works among men with God Stories, testimonies, and Kisses from Heaven from our own lives?

Yet, despite our failures, He has committed Himself to us for no valid reason beyond merciful redemption for reconciliation, given His only begotten Son to save us from His own wrath, and then kept a door open to His eternal presence by simply asking His very creation, humankind, to believe in Him as God. For that, this world mocks Him for acting as if He were God, persecutes His children for not approving sin or exalting sinners, and reliably takes vengeance against any person, place, or thing that tries to take away the lofty, self-exalted "final say in all things" that humans so often insist belongs to them alone but never to Him.

So why are we surprised or offended this world overflows with pain when He is ignored as our Comforter, full of lies when He is the Truth-Giver, addictions when He is the Deliverer, wickedness when He is our righteousness, depression when He is the Joy-Giver, peace when He is the Prince of Peace, love when He is the Lover of our Souls, and, sadly, on and on? Ultimately, must we not assign humankind's obstinate fallen nature and corporate unsaved soul as reasons for this sorrowful state?

Still, we can take heart, for there will always be a holy remnant of praying Christians in every setting who believe and long to become a recognized landing zone for His presence, lodging for His Holy Spirit, a vessel to disperse His mercy. When a body of believers, gathering together as the Spirit-filled ecclesia, are hungry to see the lost of this world transformed into saints by His undeserved salvation of grace (unmerited favor), we will see many saved, healed, delivered, and set free from the prison of sin-soaked lives.

And because He will never deny Himself the opportunity to be a good Father (Abba), brotherly Son (Jesus), and companion Friend (Holy Spirit), He does all He can to integrate His life with all humanity willing to receive it while pouring out Kisses from Heaven to convince us to trust Him, to believe His Word, and to prove His gospel by way of those unique, inexplicable, extraordinary, or supernatural testimonies (often God Stories like you have recently digested from this book) to the remainder of humankind.

If you already know Him intimately, then you have had a spiritual encounter with the God of the Universe, understand His marvelous ways, and have gleaned encouragement from this little tome of Kisses from Heaven. If you do not know Him and wish to open your life to His love, intimacy, and wonders, merely ask Jesus, and He will take you into a new way of life by way of a new birth, this time a spiritual one from Heaven. So if you make His way the best decision of your life (to be followed by your first Kiss from Heaven), take time beforehand to understand, believe in your heart, and, finally, confess with faith to the courts of Heaven what you are about to read aloud below.

Dear Father in Heaven, I believe that Jesus is the Son of God and came in loving obedience to take full punishment for all my sins so you, Father, could forgive and welcome me into your family as your child. I believe you raised Jesus from the dead so I, too, might walk in the newness of life according to your promise: "If any man is in Christ, He is a new creature; the old things passed away; behold, new things have come" (2 Cor. 5:17).

So, Father, as I have confessed Jesus as Lord and believe that You raised Him from the dead, I now receive your forgiveness, your Son's salvation, and my new life in the Spirit. Thank you, Father, thank you, Jesus, and thank you, Holy Spirit, in whose names I pray. Amen.

Dear Saint, welcome to the kingdom of Heaven and to the Church of the Living God! So blessed to know and love you with the love of our Lord, who lives within us by His Spirit, through us to fulfill His purposes, and aims to be our best friend and mentor.

In Jesus,

Caleb and Emily

Enjoy the following preview of
Kisses from Heaven Book Three

A Water Landing (1965)

The fire warning light on the Skyhawk's instrument panel blazed along with an alarm and the onset of distinct explosions aft of the cockpit. Securing the engine while deploying the emergency generator, I placed the bird, now without power, in a wings-level 250-knot descent to keep the aircraft flying.

Enveloped within a smoke-filled cockpit while furiously transmitting the details of the emergency and our present position from the ship, the message proved accurate but delivered by a voice terse, frenetic, and an octave higher than I was accustomed (a condition commonly described as "Pucker factor" by aviators). Fortunately, the carrier received my location as eighteen miles from the ship on a specified radial (bearing from the ship). Despite the cloud of intensely irritating opaque smoke severely limiting my vision, I robotically regurgitated the required actions ingrained by years of repetitive practice responding to simulated emergency conditions, this one "Fire Warning Light and Smoke in the Cockpit."

As if riding Strangelove's bomb (due to the proximity of an onboard fire to the aircraft's main fuel tank) was not enough, without warning, the aircraft's stick moved violently starboard and forward, ripping itself from my hand, and, as hard as I tried, could not be convinced to change positions, With that move, the aircraft became uncontrollable due, I suspected, to erosion of the pressurized hydraulic lines by the fire. With the airspeed exceeding 250 knots, my altimeter was rapidly winding down toward 5000 feet. The Skyhawk was on fire, unresponsive, out of control, and approaching the prescribed minimum altitude for ejection during an emergency . . .

About the Authors

Following earlier years as a Marine aviator stationed aboard the aircraft carrier USS Independence patrolling the Mediterranean Sea, participating in the Vietnam conflict, and as flight surgeon for the US Fighter Weapons School (Top Gun) in Miramar, California, C.B. "Caleb" Woodworth went on to serve as a general and emergency physician in small-town Oregon and later as award-winning Director of the Eugene Department of Veterans Affairs Clinic.

With intercessor wife Emily Anne, the couple has ministered over the last twenty-five years as ordained pastors and missionaries in restoration (inner healing) ministry among the nations. Amid struggling addicts seeking new lives in Jesus, the Woodworths presently serve as on-call volunteers with Jimi and Ladonna Waggoner's anointed Crossroads Recovery Ministry in Poplar Bluff, Missouri.

In her time, Emily helps keep those ties that bind among family, friends, and the Church while bringing in the afflicted, wounded, and needy for Holy Spirit's sozo care as an on-call listening prayer minister with husband Caleb. Her "spare" time is spent sewing, doing crafts, and living up to her reputation as the neighborhood's "cookie lady."

You will find Caleb's days reliably filled with chronicling the Lord's mysterious ways, working in the couples' Face to Face and Listening Prayer ministries, and caring for gentle Skipper and Pony (elderly equines the couple serves as fellow honored guests on Jerry and Sandra Murphy's Moriah Ranch in Missouri). Then, coaxed by insistent rooster Buc-Buc to a morning's breakfast, followed by feeding

Mommy Kitty and her ever-burgeoning number of feline progeny, it is time to be eternally nudged by overly loved Princess Peaches n' Cream Barksalot, their not-so-gracefully aging mostly Jack Russell terrier whose genes have been gratefully toned down by a competing history of pug and beagle—which must be heralded, at least by us, as an unmerited "Kiss from Heaven" by itself.

Emily and Caleb doubt the Lord could be more gracious or life sweeter in their later years. But, of course, they are open and ready for anything more from their First Love. Be certain of that.

To connect with the authors or place an order for bulk copies, please visit http://www.kissesfromheavenbooks.com.